Quick Reference Guide

Karl Schwartz/Angelo Cassano

Dictation Disc Company
14 East 38 Street, New York, NY 10016

Copyright 1991 by Dictation Disc Company

Published by Dictation Disc Company

All rights reserved, including the right to reproduce this book or portions thereof in any form whatsoever. For information, address Dictation Disc Company, 14 East 38th Street, New York, New York 10016.

First Dictation Disc Printing

ISBN: 1-56243-012-2

10 9 8 7 6 5 4 3 2

Printed in the United States of America

INTRODUCTION

The DDC Quick Reference Guide for Microsoft® MS-DOS Version 5.0 will save you hours of searching through technical manuals for directions.

Important MS-DOS terms and concepts are explained in simple language.

We've included a section on how to use the exciting new MS-DOS Shell program.

For your convenience, we've listed MS-DOS commands in alphabetical order. Command procedures are made of easy-to-follow, step-by-step instructions that tell how to execute steps from MS-DOS Shell and from the DOS prompt.

To make using MS-DOS even easier, we've included helpful notes and examples.

This book also includes an appendix that contains additional information (such as Key Commands, MS-DOS Error Messages, and Customizing MS-DOS) to help you get the most out of MS-DOS.

Authors
Karl Schwartz
Angelo Cassano

Advisors
Peter McCarthy
Joanne Schwartz

Editors
Paul Berube
Kristen Cassereau

Design and Layout
Karl Schwartz

TABLE OF CONTENTS

MS-DOS COMMANDS

USING THIS BOOK

Command Line vs. MS-DOS Shell

You may use the MS-DOS Shell program or the Command Line to execute many commands. In the MS-DOS Commands section, steps are listed as shown:

FROM MS-DOS SHELL

■ ***Command description:***

- MS-DOS Shell step-by-step procedures are listed in a box.

OR **OR**

FROM DOS PROMPT

■ ***Command description:***

- Command line step-by-step procedures are listed below the command description.

When a step contains letters in keyboard style, such as [A] [:], you must type them exactly as shown. In this case you would type A:.

NOTE: Our keyboard-style letters are capitals, but you may type either capital or lower case letters.

Some command steps show boldfaced words like **filename.ext**, **drv**, or **\path** instead of showing keyboard-style letters. These are called **substitution words** (page 3). You must substitute your own filename, drive, or directory name for them. For example, when you see **filename.ext**, you might type COINS.DAT.

Executing Procedures with the Mouse or Keyboard

HOW TO USE A MOUSE

To ***click on*** *a specified item, move mouse until pointer contacts item, then quickly press and release left mouse button.*

To ***double-click on*** *a specified item, move mouse until pointer contacts item, then press and release left mouse button twice in rapid succession.*

HOW TO INTERPRET INSTRUCTIONS USING A MOUSE OR KEYBOARD

In most cases, the procedures in this book can be used by both mouse and keyboard users, as in the following example:

1. Select Directory Tree area .... Tab

   To ***select*** *this item,* ***mouse users*** *would* ***click on*** *the Directory Tree area while* ***keyboard users*** *would press TAB until the Directory Tree area is selected.*

We use **SEPARATE KEYBOARD/MOUSE** instructions (in a few cases) when the mouse and keyboard steps are very different.

MOUSE SHORTCUTS are shown in the following format:

Mouse Shortcut: *Double-click on...*

Substitution Words

The four substitution words in the left column of this table appear throughout this guide. Whenever you see one in a command step, you must replace it according to the instructions below.

drv	Substitute a disk or diskette drive letter. *Examples:* `A` `C`

\path	Substitute a path that specifies a directory location.
	Examples: `\CLIENTS`
	`\MOM\CHILD1`
	`\FRUIT\FIG\JAM`

filename.ext	Substitute the name of a single file, including its extension (if any). Never use wildcards when replacing this substitution word. *Examples:* `DDCBOOK.LST` `YOURFILE.DOC`

filespec	Substitute a filespec (file specification) that includes **wildcard** characters.
	Examples: `*.*`
	`CHAPT??.DOC`
	`*.DOC`
	*NOTE: The **wildcard** characters are:*
	** — stands for any consecutive characters;*
	? — stands for any single character.

USING MS-DOS SHELL

MS-DOS Shell is a program that lets you work easily with disks, directories, programs and files. Some of the advantages of working with MS-DOS Shell are that you can:

- change current disk drive by choosing from drive icons;
- change current directory from the Directory Tree window;
- select files from the File list;
- choose commands from a menu;
- run programs from a program list; and
- switch between running programs.

Starting MS-DOS Shell from the DOS Prompt

MS-DOS Shell may run automatically when your computer is started if the DOSSHELL command is contained in your autoexec.bat file. *See APPENDIX — About autoexec.bat, page 128.*

FROM DOS PROMPT:

1. Type .... D O S S H E L L
2. **Enter** .... ↵

NOTE: *If your computer uses floppy disks only, insert the floppy disk containing the MS-DOS Shell program in the disk drive of your choice, then execute steps 1 and 2.*

Parts of the MS-DOS Shell Window

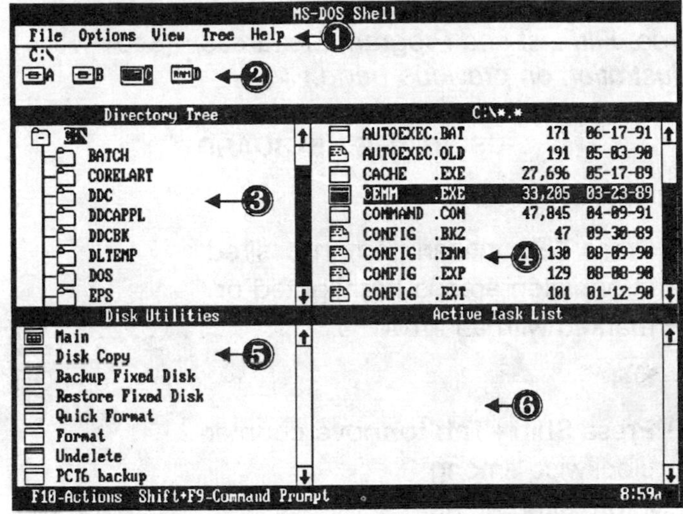

1. **Menu bar** displays menu names. A selected menu name will display a pull-down menu of commands from which you can choose.
2. **Drive List area** contains icons (pictures) of your computer's available disk drives.
3. **Directory Tree area** shows the structure of the directories on the current disk drive.
4. **File List area** shows a list of files contained in the current directory.
5. **Program List area** shows a list of installed programs that you can start directly from MS-DOS Shell.
6. **Active Task List area** shows a list of running applications. This area will not be displayed unless you have selected the Enable Task Swapper command.

Selecting Information Areas

Information areas include the Disk Drive, Directory Tree, File List and Program List areas. *(See illustration on previous page.)*

USING THE KEYBOARD

FROM ANY AREA:

1. Press **Tab** until an item in desired information area is highlighted or marked with an arrow . . . . 

   OR **OR**

   Press **Shift+Tab** to move counter-clockwise among information areas . . . . 

OR **USING A MOUSE** **OR**

1. Click on any item in desired information area.

   NOTE: Selecting an item in any information area makes the area active.

Changing Views in MS-DOS Shell

The commands that follow tell MS-DOS Shell how to show files, directories and programs.

Single File List — shows Directory Tree area and File List area.

Dual File Lists — shows two windows (one above the other). Each window contains a Directory Tree and a File List. Files on a different drive or directory can be shown in each window.

All Files — shows all files for current drive and expanded information about the selected file.

Program/File Lists — shows Directory Tree, File List and Program List areas.

Program List — shows only the Program List area.

FROM ANY AREA:

1. Select **V**iew menu . . . . Alt, V
2. Select **one** of the following: **Option**
   - **S**ingle File List . . . . S
   - **D**ual File Lists . . . . D
   - **A**ll Files . . . . A
   - Program/**F**ile Lists . . . . F
   - **P**rogram List . . . . P

About Menu Information

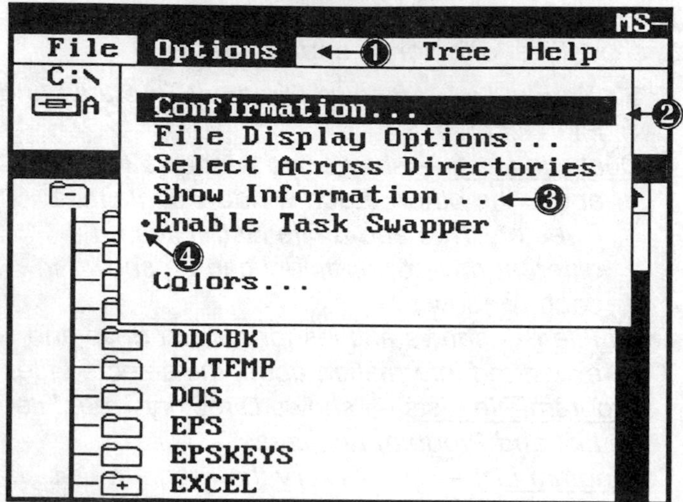

1. **Highlighted menu name**, when selected, will open to show command names on a pull-down menu.
2. **Highlighted command item** is selected by pressing Enter. You may also type the underscored letter to select a command name (e.g., type S to select "**S**how Information...").
3. **Ellipses** (...) next to a command name indicate that a **dialog box** will appear when the command is chosen. Dialog boxes are used by commands that need additional information.
4. **Diamond** (♦) before a command name indicates that the command is **active**.

Selecting a Drive

When the current drive is changed, information in the Directory Tree and File List areas will also change to show contents of the newly selected drive.

USING THE KEYBOARD

If necessary, press **Tab** until Drive List area is selected . . . . [Tab]

NOTE: The current disk drive will be highlighted.

FROM DRIVE LIST AREA:

1. • Press **Right** or **Left** arrow until desired drive icon is highlighted . . . . [←] or [→]
   • **Enter** . . . . [↵]

OR **OR**

1. • Press **Ctrl + letter** of drive to select . . . . [Ctrl] **+ letter**

   For example, press Ctrl+A to select drive A.

OR **USING A MOUSE** **OR**

1. Double-click on drive icon in Drive List area to select.

Selecting a Directory or Subdirectory

Each drive contains a root directory in which first-level directories are displayed. Directories that contain subdirectories will have a (+) before their names. The current directory, in the Directory Tree Area, is highlighted or marked with an arrow.

FROM DIRECTORY TREE AREA:

To select a directory:

USING THE KEYBOARD

1. Press **Up** or **Down** arrow until directory to select is highlighted . . . . ↑ or ↓

OR **USING A MOUSE** **OR**

1. Click on directory name to select.

   If directory name is not in view, click on Up or Down scroll arrow, then execute step 1.

To select a subdirectory of current directory:

USING THE KEYBOARD

1. • Press **+** (plus sign) . . . . +
   (to display subdirectories)

   • Press **Down** arrow until subdirectory to select is highlighted . . . . ↓

OR **USING A MOUSE** **OR**

1. • Click on plus sign (+) before directory name to display subdirectories.

   • Click on subdirectory name to select.

Expanding/Collapsing View of Subdirectories

A directory that contains one or more subdirectories will have a plus sign (+) before its name. Use the commands below to show or hide the display of subdirectories in the Directory Tree area.

Expand One Level — shows next level subdirectory.
Expand Branch — shows all subdirectories for the current directory.
Expand All — shows all subdirectories for all directories in Directory Tree.
Collapse Branch — removes view of subdirectories for current directory.

FROM DIRECTORY TREE AREA:

1. Select directory to expand/collapse. (Press **Up** or **Down** arrow until a directory with a (+) or (-) sign is highlighted.) ↑ or ↓
2. Select **T**ree menu . . . . Alt, T
3. Select **one** of the following: **Option**
   - E**x**pand One Level X
   - Expand **B**ranch . . . . B
   - Expand **A**ll . . . . A
   - **C**ollapse Branch C

Mouse Shortcut: *Click on plus sign (+) before directory name to expand. Click on minus sign (-) before directory name to collapse.*

Updating Display in the File List Area

Information in the File List area may not be up-to-date. This can occur when you leave MS-DOS Shell and make changes to files.

FROM DIRECTORY TREE AREA:

1. Select directory to update .... ↑ or ↓
   (Press **Up** or **Down** arrow until
   directory to update is highlighted.)
2. • Select **V**iew menu .... Alt, V
   • Select Re**p**aint Screen .... E

   OR **OR**

   • Press **Shift+F5** .... Shift + F5

Updating Display of Disk Information for Current Drive

If disk drive to be used reads diskettes, insert desired diskette before using this command.

FROM DIRECTORY, FILE, OR DRIVE LIST AREA:

1. Select **V**iew menu .... Alt, V
2. Select **R**efresh .... R

OR **OR**

1. Press **F5** F5

Mouse Shortcut: Double-click on current disk drive icon in Drive List area.

Changing the File List Display

Use these commands to view specific groups of files and to change the sort order of files displayed.

FROM DIRECTORY TREE OR FILE LIST AREA:

1. Select **O**ptions menu . . . . Alt, O
2. Select **F**ile Display Options... . . . . F

FROM "FILE DISPLAY OPTIONS" DIALOG BOX:

▪ *To show a specific file or group of files:*

a) Type a filename in the "Name" text box.

OR

a) Type a filespec in the "Name" text box.

NOTE: For example, type <u>*.DOC</u> *to show only files with a .DOC filename extension.*

b) Execute step 3 or choose another option.

▪ *To show hidden and system files:*

USING THE KEYBOARD

a) • Press **Tab** until underscore appears in "Display hidden/system files" check box . . . . Tab

• Press **Space** to select . . . . SPACE

OR **USING A MOUSE** **OR**

a) Click on "Display hidden/system files" check box to select.

b) Execute step 3 or choose another option.

Continued ...

■ *To show files in descending order:*

USING THE KEYBOARD

a) • Press **Tab** until underscore appears in "Descending order" check box . . . . Tab

• Press **Space** to select . . . . SPACE

OR **USING A MOUSE** **OR**

a) Click on "Descending order" check box to select.

b) Execute step 3 or choose another option.

■ *To change sort order of files:*

USING THE KEYBOARD

a) • Press **Tab** until "sort by:" group is selected . . . . Tab

• Press **Up** or **Down** arrow to select desired option button . . ↑ or ↓

OR **USING A MOUSE** **OR**

a) Click on desired option button in "sort by:" group.

3. Select **OK** . . . . ↵

Selecting Files in the File List Area

Select files or groups of files before using file commands such as Move, Copy, and Delete.

■ *To select one file:*

USING THE KEYBOARD

1. Press **Tab** until File List area is selected . . . . [Tab]

   NOTE: The first file in list is highlighted.

2. Press **Up** or **Down** arrow until desired file is highlighted . . . . [↑] or [↓]

OR USING A MOUSE OR

1. Click on desired file in File List area.

   If filename is not in view, click on Up or Down scroll arrow, then execute step 1.

■ *To select files listed in sequence:*

FROM FILE LIST AREA:

USING THE KEYBOARD

1. Press **Up** or **Down** arrow until first file to select is highlighted . . . . [↑] or [↓]
2. Press and hold **Shift** while pressing **Up** or **Down** arrow . . [Shift] + [↑] or [↓] (to extend selection).

OR USING A MOUSE OR

1. Click on first file to select.
2. Press and hold **Shift** while clicking on last file in sequence to select.

Continued ...

■ *To select files not listed in sequence:*

FROM FILE LIST AREA:

USING THE KEYBOARD

1. Press **Up** or **Down** arrow until first file to select is highlighted . . . . ↑ or ↓
2. Press **Shift+F8** to **begin** "Add" mode . . . . Shift + F8
3. Press **Up** or **Down** arrow until next file to select is highlighted . . . . ↑ or ↓
4. Press **Space** to select . . . . SPACE
5. Repeat steps 3 and 4 for each file to select.
6. Press **Shift+F8** to **end** "Add" mode . . Shift + F8

OR **USING A MOUSE** **OR**

1. Press and hold **Ctrl** while clicking on **each** file to select.

■ *To select all files:*

FROM FILE LIST AREA:

1. Select **F**ile menu . . . . Alt, F
2. Select **S**elect All . . . . S

Canceling File Selections

■ *To cancel any single file selection:*

FROM FILE LIST AREA:

- Select any other file . . . . ↑ or ↓

■ *To cancel selections from an extended file selection:*

FROM FILE LIST AREA:

USING THE KEYBOARD

If necessary, press **Shift+F8** to **begin** "Add" mode . . . . Shift + F8

1. Press **Up** or **Down** arrow until file to deselect is outlined . . . . ↑ or ↓
2. Press **Space** . . . . SPACE
3. Press **Shift+F8** to **end** "Add" mode . . Shift + F8

   NOTE: While in "Add" mode, pressing the Spacebar will alternately select or deselect the current file.

OR **USING A MOUSE** **OR**

1. Press **Ctrl** while clicking on any selected file.

■ *To cancel all file selections:*

FROM FILE LIST AREA:

1. Select **F**ile menu . . . . Alt, F
2. Select Dese**l**ect All L

   NOTE: The first selected file will remain selected.

Showing Expanded Information About a Selected File, Drive, and Directory

FROM FILE, DRIVE, OR DIRECTORY LIST AREA:

1. Select **O**ptions menu . . . . Alt, O
2. Select **S**how Information... . . . . S
3. Read information about selected file, drive, or directory.
4. Select **Close** . . . . 

About the Program List

Use the Program List to run applications installed on your system. The program list contains PROGRAM GROUPS (Application folders) and PROGRAM ITEMS (Applications). By default, the Program List displays the Main group. The Main group contains the following program items: Command Prompt, Editor, and MS-DOS QBasic. The Main group also contains the Disk Utilities program group. You may add as many program groups and program items as you like to the Program List area.

Viewing the Program List

MS-DOS Shell is preset to show the Program List area in the bottom-left section of the screen. If the Program List area is not in view, see Changing Views in MS-DOS Shell, page 7, for information about displaying the Program List.

Opening a Program Group

Open a program group to run applications the group contains. Program group names are displayed in brackets or with a group icon

FROM PROGRAM LIST AREA:

USING THE KEYBOARD

1. Press **Up** or **Down** arrow until desired group name is highlighted . . . . ↑ or ↓
2. **Enter** . . . . ↵

OR **USING A MOUSE** **OR**

1. Double-click on desired group name.

   If group name is not in view, click on Up or Down scroll arrow, then execute step 1.

NOTE: If a group is not found in the current list, it may be located inside another group. You can open the ***previous group*** *by pressing Home, Up, then Enter or by double-clicking on the group name at top of the list.*

Starting Programs from MS-DOS Shell

There are three ways to run a program from MS-DOS Shell: from the Program List area, from the File List area, and by using the Run command.

■ *To start a program from the Program List area:*

USING THE KEYBOARD

If necessary, press **Tab** until Program List area is selected . . . . Tab

NOTE: A program item in the list will be highlighted.

FROM PROGRAM LIST AREA:

If necessary, open group containing program to run (page 19).

1. Press **Up** or **Down** arrow until program to run is highlighted . . . . . ↑ or ↓
2. **Enter** . . . . ↵

OR **USING A MOUSE** **OR**

If necessary, open group containing program to run (page 19).

1. Double-click on program name to run.

Continued ...

■ *To start a program from the File List area:*

FROM FILE LIST AREA:

USING THE KEYBOARD

1. Press **Up** or **Down** arrow until program file or associated data file is highlighted. ↑ or ↓

   See Associating Programs with Data Files, page 22.

2. **Enter** . . . . ↵

OR **USING A MOUSE** **OR**

1. Double-click on desired program file or associated data file to run.

   See Associating Programs with Data Files, page 22.

■ *To start a program with the Run Command:*

FROM ANY AREA:

1. Select **F**ile menu . . . . Alt, F
2. Select **R**un... . . . . R

FROM "RUN" DIALOG BOX:

To run a program in current directory or path list:

- Type complete program name.

  For example, type `WP.EXE`

To run a program that is not in current directory or path list:

- Type the drive, path and program name.

  For example, type `C:\WP51\WP.EXE`

3. Select **OK** . . . . ↵

Associating Programs with Data Files

This will link a specified program with data files that have the same filename extension. This allows MS-DOS Shell to start an application and open a data file in one step.

FROM FILE LIST AREA:

1. Select desired program or data file. . [↑] or [↓]
   (Press **Up** or **Down** arrow until
   program or data file is highlighted.)

   NOTE: Only programs that provide for loading of data files from the DOS command prompt will load associated data files from MS-DOS Shell.

2. Select **F**ile menu . . . . [Alt], [F]
3. Select **A**ssociate... . . . . [A]

FROM "ASSOCIATE FILE" DIALOG BOX:

IF selected file is a program file:

- Type filename extension(s) in "Extensions" text box. Separate each extension with a space.
  For example, type `DOC WP5`

  NOTE: Do not type periods.

IF selected file is a data file:

- Type drive, path and program name in text box.
  For example, type `C:\WP51\WP.EXE`

4. Select **OK** . . . . [↵]

Searching for Files

Locates specific files or groups of files on the current drive.

FROM DIRECTORY TREE OR FILE LIST AREA:

1. Select **F**ile menu .... Alt, F
2. Select Search... .... H

FROM "SEARCH FILE" DIALOG BOX:

To specify files to find:

3. • Type complete filename.

   For example, type YOURFILE.DOC

   OR

   • Type a filespec.

   For example, type *.DOC

   NOTE: A filespec uses wildcards (,?) to refer to any characters in a filename.*

   To search only current directory:

   USING THE KEYBOARD

   • Press **Tab** to move to "Search entire disk" check box .... Tab
   • Press **Space** to deselect option ... 

   OR **USING A MOUSE** **OR**

   • Click on "Search entire disk" check box to deselect.

4. Select **OK** .... ↵

NOTE: A search result window appears. Perform desired action or press Esc to return to information area.

About Task Swapper

Use Task Swapper to switch between running applications. For example, you can run a word processing program, return to MS-DOS Shell (without exiting the program) and then run a spreadsheet program. Now with one keystroke, you can switch between these running programs.

Starting/Disabling Task Swapper

When Task Swapper is on, a diamond appears to the left of the command name in the pull-down menu, and the Active Task List area appears in the lower-right side of the screen. Running applications will be displayed in this list.

FROM ANY AREA:

1. Select **O**ptions menu . . . . Alt, O
2. Select **E**nable Task Swapper . . . . E

Running More than One Application

FROM ANY AREA:

If necessary, start Task Swapper (above).

1. Start the first program (pages 20,21).
2. Press **Ctrl+Esc** to return to MS-DOS Shell . . . . Ctrl+Esc

   NOTE: The first program started will appear on the Active Task List.
3. Start another program.

Switching Between Running Applications

NOTE: You must start Task Swapper (page 24) to run more than one application.

■ *To switch to another program from MS-DOS Shell:*

FROM ACTIVE TASK LIST AREA:

USING THE KEYBOARD

1. Press **Up** or **Down** arrow until program to run is highlighted .... ↑ or ↓
2. **Enter** .... ↵

OR **USING A MOUSE** **OR**

1. Double-click on program name to run in Active Task List.

■ *To switch to another program from any program:*

USING THE KEYBOARD

1. Press and hold **Alt** .... Alt
2. Press **Tab** .... Tab

   Do not release **Alt** key and allow time for program name to be displayed.

   If desired program name is not displayed,
   - Continue to press **Tab** until name of desired running program appears on screen .... Tab
3. Release **Alt** key.

Continued ...

▪ *To switch to MS-DOS Shell from any program:*

- Press **Ctrl+Esc** .... Ctrl + Esc

OR OR

- Press **Alt+Tab** .... Alt + Tab

Removing Programs from the Active Task List

▪ *To remove running programs from the Active Task List:*

1. Switch to program to be removed. (See Switching Between Running Applications, page 25.)
2. Use program's quit command.

▪ *To remove locked up programs from the Active Task List:*

FROM ACTIVE TASK LIST AREA:

1. Select program that has locked up .... ↑ or ↓
   (Press **Up** or **Down** arrow until program that has locked up is highlighted.)
2. Select **F**ile menu .... Alt , F
3. Select **D**elete .... D

   NOTE: *When a program locks up, quit all running programs (if possible), then turn your system off and start over.*

Adding a Program Group to the Program List

Add program groups (application folders) to help organize programs installed on your system. If Program List area is not in view, select the Program/File Lists command. (See Changing Views in MS-DOS Shell, page 7.)

FROM PROGRAM LIST AREA:

1. Select **F**ile menu . . . . Alt, F
2. Select **N**ew... . . . . N

FROM "NEW PROGRAM OBJECT" DIALOG BOX:

3. Select "Program Group" option button . . . . ↑
4. Select **OK** . . . . ↵

FROM "ADD GROUP" DIALOG BOX:

5. Type a program group name in "Title" text box.

   To add a help message:

   - Select "Help Text" text box . . . . Tab
     (Press **Tab** until text box is selected.)
   - Type a message in text box.

   To add a password:

   - Select "Password" text box . . . . Tab
     (Press **Tab** until text box is selected.)
   - Type a password in text box.

6. Select **OK** . . . . ↵

Adding a Program Item to the Program List

You may add program items (applications) to any program group (application folder). If Program List area is not in view, select the Program/File Lists command. (See Changing Views in MS-DOS Shell, page 7.)

FROM PROGRAM LIST AREA:

1. Select **F**ile menu .... Alt, F
2. Select **N**ew... .... N

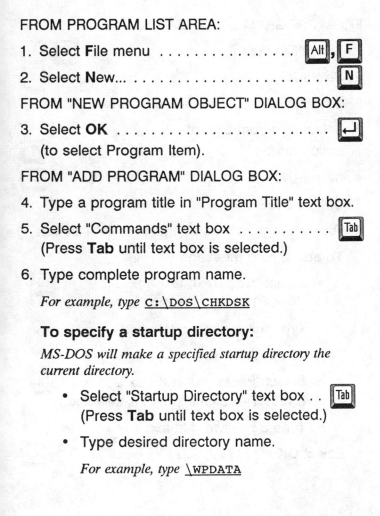

FROM "NEW PROGRAM OBJECT" DIALOG BOX:

3. Select **OK** .... ↵
   (to select Program Item).

FROM "ADD PROGRAM" DIALOG BOX:

4. Type a program title in "Program Title" text box.
5. Select "Commands" text box .... Tab
   (Press **Tab** until text box is selected.)
6. Type complete program name.

   For example, type C:\DOS\CHKDSK

   To specify a startup directory:

   MS-DOS will make a specified startup directory the current directory.

   - Select "Startup Directory" text box . . 
     (Press **Tab** until text box is selected.)
   - Type desired directory name.

     For example, type \WPDATA

Continued ...

To assign an application shortcut key:

MS-DOS will switch to this program (if it is running) when assigned key is pressed.

- Select "Application Shortcut Key" text box . . . . 
  (Press **Tab** until text box is selected.)
- Type a Shortcut key.

  For example, type CTRL+W

To deselect "Pause after exit" check box:

If this option remains selected, you will not return immediately to MS-DOS Shell when program is finished.

- Deselect "Pause after exit" check box . . . . Tab, SPACE
  (Press **Tab** until cursor moves to check box, then press Space to deselect.)

To assign a password:

- Select "Password" text box . . . . Tab
  (Press **Tab** until text box is selected.)
- Type a password.

7. Select **OK** . . . . 

   NOTE: If a replaceable parameter code was typed, an additional "Add Program:" dialog box appears. (For information about this dialog box, see Including a Replaceable Parameter in a Startup Command for a Program Item, pages 31,32.)

Changing Properties of a Program Item or Program Group

FROM PROGRAM LIST AREA:

1. Select program item or group to change .... ↑ or ↓
   (Press **Up** or **Down** arrow until desired program item or group is highlighted.)
2. Select **F**ile menu .... Alt, F
3. Select **P**roperties... .... P

FROM "PROGRAM ITEM OR GROUP PROPERTIES" DIALOG BOX:

4. Select information area to change .... Tab
   (Press **Tab** until desired text box is selected.)
5. Type new information in text box.
6. Repeat steps 4 and 5 for each information area to change.
7. Select **OK** .... ↵

Including a Replaceable Parameter in a Startup Command for a Program Item

A replaceable parameter, such as %1, added to the end of a startup command tells MS-DOS to provide a "prompt" dialog box when the program is run.

FROM PROGRAM LIST AREA:

1. Select program item to change .... ↑ or ↓
   (Press **Up** or **Down** arrow until program item to change is highlighted.)
2. Select **F**ile menu .... Alt, F
3. Select **P**roperties... .... P

FROM "PROGRAM ITEM PROPERTIES" DIALOG BOX:

4. Select "Commands" text box .... Tab
   (Press **Tab** until text box is selected.)
5. Type a space after program name, then type a replaceable parameter code (%1-9).
   For example, type C:\WP51\WP %1
6. Select **OK** .... ↵

FROM "PROGRAM ITEM PROPERTIES" DIALOG BOX:

a) Select appropriate text box .... Tab
   (Press **Tab** until desired text box is selected.)

b) Type information in text box.

c) Repeat steps a and b for each item.

7. Select **OK** .... ↵

Continued ...

The illustration below shows how information typed in the "Program Item Properties" dialog box (top) is applied to the WordPerfect dialog box (bottom). The program prompt dialog box is displayed when you run the program to which the "Program Item Properties" box belongs.

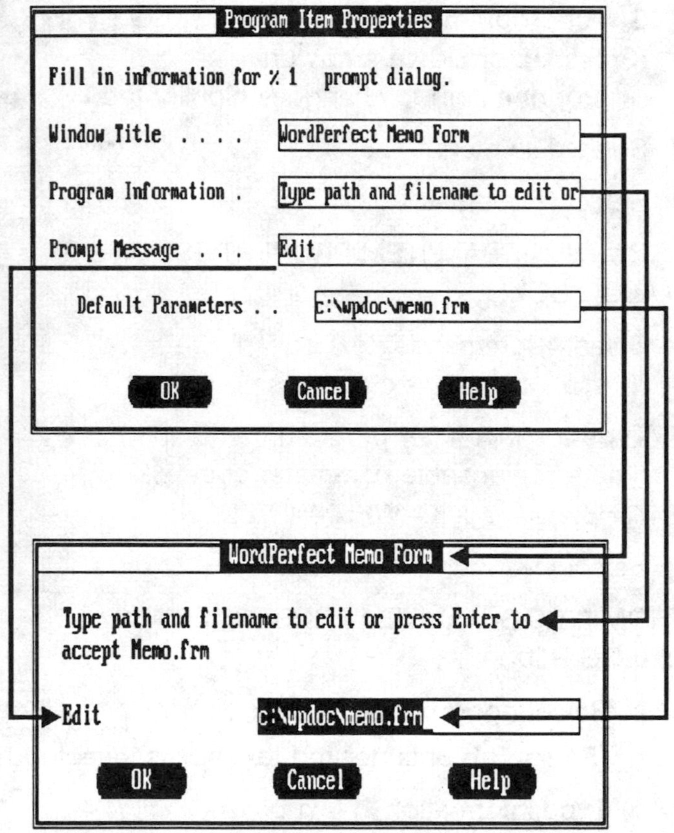

Calling Batch Programs in a Startup Command for a Program Item

Batch programs are files containing groups of DOS commands.

FROM PROGRAM LIST AREA:

1. Select program item to change .... [↑] or [↓]
   (Press **Up** or **Down** arrow until program item to change is highlighted.)
2. Select **F**ile menu .... [Alt], [F]
3. Select **P**roperties... .... [P]

FROM "PROGRAM ITEM PROPERTIES" DIALOG BOX:

4. Select "Commands" text box .... [Tab]
   (Press **Tab** until text box is selected.)
5. Place cursor before or after program name.
6. Type a CALL command.

   NOTE: *Type a space and a semicolon (;) between each command item.*

   Example: `CALL cKspc ; wp ; CALL cpdoc`

   This example shows batch files named CKSPC and CPDOC that are called, respectively, before and after the program WP is run.
7. Select **OK** .... [↵]

Deleting Program Items and Program Groups

Program groups containing program items cannot be deleted.

FROM PROGRAM LIST AREA:

1. Select program group or program item to delete . . . . [↑] or [↓]
   (Press **Up** or **Down** arrow until program group or program item to delete is highlighted.)

2. • Select **F**ile menu . . . . [Alt], [F]
   • Select **D**elete . . . . [D]

   OR **OR**

   • Press **Del** . . . . [Del]

3. Select **OK** . . . . [↵]

Changing the Order of Program Items and Program Groups

FROM PROGRAM LIST AREA:

1. Select program item or group to move . . . . ↑ or ↓
   (Press **Up** or **Down** arrow until program item or group to move is highlighted.)
2. Select **F**ile menu . . . . Alt, F
3. Select Reor**d**er . . . . E

USING THE KEYBOARD

4. • Press **Up** or **Down** arrow until new location is highlighted . . . . . ↑ or ↓
   • **Enter** . . . . ↵

OR **USING A MOUSE** **OR**

4. • Double-click on new location.

Copying a Program Item to Another Program Group

FROM PROGRAM LIST AREA:

1. Select program item to copy .... ↑ or ↓
   (Press **Up** or **Down** arrow until program item to copy is highlighted.)
2. Select **F**ile menu .... Alt, F
3. Select **C**opy C
4. Open program group to which program item is to be copied (page 19).
5. Press **F2** F2

NOTE: To move a program item, delete original program item after copying it. (See Deleting Program Items and Program Groups, page 34.)

Temporarily Leaving MS-DOS Shell

FROM ANY AREA:

USING THE KEYBOARD

- Press **Shift+F9** . . . . Shift + F9

OR **USING A MOUSE** **OR**

FROM PROGRAM LIST AREA — MAIN GROUP:

- Double-click on Command Prompt program.

Returning to MS-DOS Shell from the Command Prompt

FROM DOS PROMPT:

1. Type EXIT . . . . E X I T
2. **Enter** . . . . ↵

Quitting MS-DOS Shell

FROM ANY AREA:

If necessary, quit each program in the Active Task List.

1. Select **F**ile menu . . . . Alt, F
2. Select Exit X

OR **OR**

1. Press **F3** F3

MS-DOS COMMANDS

This section of the book contains instructions on the following MS-DOS 5.0 commands:

APPEND

Enables programs to open files in other directories as if the files were in the current directory.

FROM DOS PROMPT

■ ***To append a directory to current directory:***

1. Type **APPEND** .... A P P E N D
2. Press **Space** .... SPACE
3. Specify drive and directory to append to current directory ... **drv** : **\path**
4. **Enter** .... ↵

   Example: APPEND C:\DATA
   Appends the DATA directory of drive C to the current working directory.

FROM DOS PROMPT

■ ***To cancel the list of appended directories:***

1. Type **APPEND;**. A P P E N D ;
2. **Enter** .... ↵

ASSIGN

Redirects disk operation requests from one disk to another.

FROM DOS PROMPT

▪ *To assign disk operations:*

1. Type **ASSIGN** ..... A S S I G N
2. Press **Space** .... SPACE
3. Specify drive to be assigned .... **drv**
4. Press = (equal sign) .... =
5. Specify drive to handle disk requests .. **drv**
6. **Enter** .... ↵

   Example: ASSIGN A=C
   Will redirect all disk requests intended for drive A to drive C.

FROM DOS PROMPT

▪ *To display a list of current drive assignments:*

1. Type **ASSIGN** ..... A S S I G N
2. Press / (slash) .... /
3. Type **STATUS** ..... S T A T U S
4. **Enter** .... ↵

   Example: ASSIGN/STATUS

Continued ...

FROM DOS PROMPT

■ ***To reset all drive letters to their original drive:***

1. Type **ASSIGN** ..... A S S I G N
2. **Enter** .... ↵

ATTRIB

A file attribute indicates limitations of how a file can be used. File attributes include:

Read-Only — prevents file from being changed.
Archive — indicates that file has been modified.
Hidden — determines if file can be listed in an MS-DOS file listing.
System — identifies files as MS-DOS system file.

FROM MS-DOS SHELL

■ ***To display or change file attributes:***

FROM FILE LIST AREA:

1. Select desired file (page 15).
2. Select **F**ile menu .... Alt, F
3. Select Chan**g**e Attributes .... G
4. Select/Deselect attributes. ↑ or ↓, SPACE
   (Press **Up** or **Down** arrow until attribute to select is highlighted, then press Space. Repeat for each attribute to change.)
5. Select **OK** .... ↵

Continued ...

OR **OR**

FROM DOS PROMPT

▩ *To display file attributes:*

1. Type **ATTRIB** ..... A T T R I B
2. Press **Space** .... SPACE
3. Specify filename .... **filename.ext**
4. **Enter** .... ↵

   Example: `ATTRIB AUTOEXEC.BAT`
   Displays all the attributes of the AUTOEXEC.BAT file.

FROM DOS PROMPT

▩ *To change file attributes:*

1. Type **ATTRIB** ..... A T T R I B
2. Press **Space** .... SPACE
3. Specify attribute .... **+letter** or **-letter**

   +a sets archive attribute — **-a** clears archive attribute
   +h sets file to hidden — **-h** clears hidden file setting
   +r sets file to read-only — **-r** clears read-only setting
   +s sets file to system file — **-s** clears system file setting
4. Press **Space** .... SPACE
5. Specify filename .... **filename.ext**
6. **Enter** .... ↵

   Example: `ATTRIB +r AUTOEXEC.BAT`
   Sets AUTOEXEC.BAT file to read-only.

Continued ...

Switches for ATTRIB command:

Switches (shown in bold) provide optional information that directs command to act in a specific way.

+a sets archive attribute

-a clears archive attribute

+h sets file to hidden

-h clears hidden file attribute

+r sets file to read-only

-r clears read-only attribute

+s sets file to a system file

-s clears system file attribute

/s processes files in current directory and all subdirectories

Command structure for ATTRIB command:

ATTRIB **+switch** or **-switch**
drv:\path\FILENAME.EXT **/s**

Example: `ATTRIB +r AUTOEXEC.BAT`
Sets the autoexec.bat file to read-only, preventing the file from being deleted or modified.

BACKUP

Backs up one or more files from one disk to another.

Warning! This command erases all files on the destination disk. Therefore do not back up to a destination disk that contains useful data.

FROM MS-DOS SHELL

■ *To back up entire hard drive:*

FROM PROGRAM LIST AREA — MAIN GROUP:

USING THE KEYBOARD

1. • Press **D** (Disk Utilities) . . . . D
   • **Enter** . . . . ↵
   • Press **B** (Backup Fixed Disk) . . . . . . B
   • **Enter** . . . . ↵

OR **USING A MOUSE** **OR**

1. • Double-click on Disk Utilities.
   • Double-click on Backup Fixed Disk.

FROM "BACKUP FIXED DISK" DIALOG BOX:

2. Specify source drive . . . . **drv** :
3. Type *.* . . . . \ * . *
   (to back up all files)
4. Press **Space** . . . . SPACE
5. Specify destination drive . . . . **drv** :
6. Press **Space** . . . . SPACE

Continued ...

To back up entire hard drive (continued):

7. Type **/S** . . . . [/] [S]
   (to back up all subdirectories)
   Example (steps 2-7): C:*.* A: /S
8. Select **OK** . . . . [↵]
9. Insert backup diskette when requested.
10. **Enter** . . . . [↵]
11. Repeat steps 9 & 10 if requested to insert another diskette.
12. **Enter** . . . . [↵]
    (to return to DOSSHELL)

OR **OR**

FROM DOS PROMPT

▪ *To back up entire hard drive:*

1. Type **BACKUP** . . . . [B] [A] [C] [K] [U] [P]
2. Press **Space** . . . . [SPACE]
3. Specify source drive . . . . drv [:]
4. Type ***.*** . . . . [\] [*] [.] [*]
   (to back up all files)
5. Press **Space** . . . . [SPACE]
6. Specify destination drive . . . . drv [:]
7. Press **Space** . . . . [SPACE]
8. Type **/S** . . . . [/] [S]
   (to back up all subdirectories)
9. **Enter** . . . . [↵]

Continued ...

10. Insert backup diskette when requested.
11. **Enter** .... [↵]
12. Repeat steps 10 & 11 if requested to insert another diskette.

    Example: BACKUP C:*.* A: /S
    Backs up the entire contents of drive C to diskette in drive A.

FROM MS-DOS SHELL

To back up a specific directory on a hard disk:

FROM PROGRAM LIST AREA — MAIN GROUP:

USING THE KEYBOARD

1. • Press **D** (Disk Utilities) .... [D]
   • **Enter** .... [↵]
   • Press **B** (Backup Fixed Disk) ...... [B]
   • **Enter** .... [↵]

OR **USING A MOUSE** **OR**

1. • Double-click on Disk Utilities.
   • Double-click on Backup Fixed Disk.

FROM "BACKUP FIXED DISK" DIALOG BOX:

2. Specify drive to back up .... **drv** [:]
3. Specify directory to back up .... **\path**

Continued ...

To back up a specific directory on a hard disk (continued):

4. Press **Space** .... SPACE
5. Specify destination drive .... **drv** :

   Example (steps 2-5): C:\WPDOC B:
6. Select **OK** .... ↵
7. Insert backup diskette when requested.
8. **Enter** .... ↵
9. Repeat steps 7 & 8 if requested to insert another diskette.
10. **Enter** .... ↵

    (to return to DOSSHELL)

OR **OR**

FROM DOS PROMPT

▩ *To back up a specific directory on a hard disk:*

1. Type **BACKUP** .... B A C K U P
2. Press **Space** .... SPACE
3. Specify drive to back up. .... **drv** :
4. Specify directory to back up .... **\path**
5. Press **Space** .... SPACE
6. Specify destination drive .... **drv** :
7. **Enter** .... ↵
8. Insert backup diskette when requested.

Continued ...

9. **Enter** .... ↵

10. Repeat steps 8 & 9 if requested to insert another diskette.

    Example: <u>BACKUP</u> <u>C:\NAMES</u> <u>A:</u>
    Backs up all files in the NAMES directory of drive C to diskette drive A.

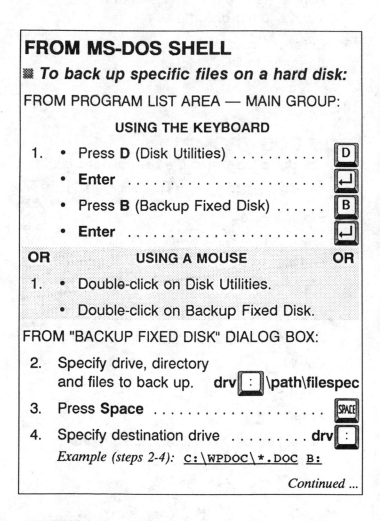

FROM MS-DOS SHELL

▩ *To back up specific files on a hard disk:*

FROM PROGRAM LIST AREA — MAIN GROUP:

USING THE KEYBOARD

1. • Press **D** (Disk Utilities) .... D
   • **Enter** .... ↵
   • Press **B** (Backup Fixed Disk) ...... B
   • **Enter** .... ↵

OR **USING A MOUSE** **OR**

1. • Double-click on Disk Utilities.
   • Double-click on Backup Fixed Disk.

FROM "BACKUP FIXED DISK" DIALOG BOX:

2. Specify drive, directory and files to back up. **drv** : **\path\filespec**

3. Press **Space** .... SPACE

4. Specify destination drive .... **drv** :

   Example (steps 2-4): <u>C:\WPDOC*.DOC</u> <u>B:</u>

Continued ...

To backup specific files on a hard disk (continued):

5. Select **OK** .... [Enter]
6. Insert backup diskette when requested.
7. **Enter** .... [Enter]
8. Repeat steps 6 & 7 if requested to insert another diskette.
9. **Enter** .... [Enter]
   (to return to DOSSHELL)

OR **OR**

FROM DOS PROMPT

To back up specific files on a hard disk:

1. Type **BACKUP** .... [B] [A] [C] [K] [U] [P]
2. Press **Space** .... [SPACE]
3. Specify drive, directory and files to back up. **drv** [:] **\path\filespec**
4. Press **Space** .... [SPACE]
5. Specify destination drive .... **drv** [:]

   Example: BACKUP C:\WPDOC*.DOC A:
6. **Enter** .... [Enter]
7. Insert backup diskette when requested.
8. **Enter** .... [Enter]
9. Repeat steps 7 & 8 if requested to insert another diskette.

Continued ...

Switches for BACKUP command:

Switches (shown in bold) provide optional information that directs command to act in a specific way.

/s	backs up all subdirectories.
/m	backs up only files that have been modified since the last backup.
/a	adds backup files to an existing backup disk without deleting existing files.
/f:size	formats the backup disk to the size specified. Available sizes: 160, 180, 320, 360, 720, 1.2, 1.44, 2.88.
/d:date	backs up files modified on or after the specified date; enter date as mm-dd-yy.
/t:time	backs up files modified on or after the specified time; enter time as hh:mm:ss.
/l	creates a log file of the backup.

Command structure for BACKUP command:

BACKUP DRV:\path\filespec DRV: **/s /m /a /f: /d: /t:**

Example: `BACKUP C:\names\*.boy A:` **`/f:`**`1.2`
Backs up all files with a BOY extension in the NAMES directory of drive C to diskette drive A and format backup diskette as specified.

Example: `BACKUP C:\names\*.boy A:` **`/s /m`**
Backs up all files that have been modified since the last backup with the extension BOY in the NAMES directory and its subdirectories of drive C to diskette drive A.

CD (CHDIR)

Changes the current directory or displays the name of the current directory.

NOTE: CHDIR and CD are interchangeable.

FROM MS-DOS SHELL

▪ *To change to a different directory:*

FROM DIRECTORY TREE AREA:

- Select desired directory .... [↑] or [↓]
  (Press **Up** or **Down** arrow until desired directory is highlighted.)

Also see Selecting a Directory or Subdirectory, page 10.

OR **OR**

FROM DOS PROMPT

▪ *To change to a different directory:*

1. Type **CD** .... [C] [D]
2. Press **Space** .... [SPACE]
3. Specify new directory .... **\path**
4. **Enter** .... [↵]

   Example: CD \DOS
   Changes the current directory to the DOS directory.

Continued ...

FROM MS-DOS SHELL

■ ***To change to a subdirectory of the current directory:***

FROM DIRECTORY TREE AREA:

1. Press + (plus sign) .... +
2. Select desired subdirectory .... ↑ or ↓
   (Press **Up** or **Down** arrow until desired subdirectory is highlighted.)

Also see Expanding/Collapsing View of Subdirectories, page 11.

OR **OR**

FROM DOS PROMPT

■ ***To change to a subdirectory of the current directory:***

1. Type **CD** .... C D
2. Press **Space** .... SPACE
3. Specify subdirectory name. **directory name**
4. **Enter** .... ↵

   Example: CD DOCS
   If current directory C:\WP51 has a subdirectory DOCS, new directory will be C:\WP51\DOCS.

Continued ...

FROM MS-DOS SHELL

▪ ***To change to parent directory of the current directory:***

FROM DIRECTORY TREE AREA:

1. Select desired parent directory. 
   (Press **Up** or **Down** arrow until desired parent directory is highlighted.)

OR **OR**

FROM DOS PROMPT

▪ ***To change to parent directory of the current directory:***

1. Type **CD..** . . . . C D . .
2. **Enter** . . . . ↵

   Example: `CD..`
   If current directory is C:\WP51\DOCS, new directory will be C:\WP51.

FROM DOS PROMPT

▪ ***To display name of current directory:***

1. Type **CD** . . . . 
2. **Enter** . . . . ↵

CHANGE DRIVE

Changes the current disk drive.

FROM MS-DOS SHELL

▪ *To make a different drive the current disk drive:*

FROM DRIVE LIST AREA:

USING THE KEYBOARD

1. Press **Left** or **Right** arrow until desired drive icon is highlighted .... [←] **or** [→]
2. **Enter** .... [↵]

OR **USING A MOUSE** **OR**

1. Double-click on desired drive icon.

OR **OR**

FROM DOS PROMPT

▪ *To make a different drive the current disk drive:*

NOTE: When making a floppy disk drive the current drive, be sure a diskette is in that drive.

1. Specify drive .... **drv** [:]
2. **Enter** .... [↵]

   Example: A: *or* B:

CHKDSK

Creates and displays a status report of disk and RAM space.

FROM DOS PROMPT

▪ ***To display total and available statistics on disk and RAM (memory) space:***

1. Type **CHKDSK** .... C H K D S K
2. Press **Space** .... SPACE
3. Specify drive .... **drv** :
4. **Enter** .... ↵

Example: `CHKDSK C:`

NOTE: *If prompted for a Yes or No response, press N and* ***Enter****. Refer to the CHKDSK command in DOS manual for further explanation of messages displayed.*

CLS (Clear Screen)

Clears the screen of all text and positions cursor in upper left corner of screen.

FROM DOS PROMPT

▪ ***To clear screen of all text:***

1. Type **CLS** .... C L S
2. **Enter** .... ↵

COPY

Copies the content of one or more files to another location.

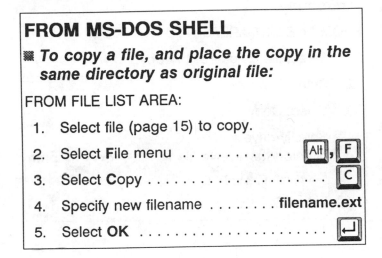

FROM MS-DOS SHELL

- ***To copy a file, and place the copy in the same directory as original file:***

FROM FILE LIST AREA:

1. Select file (page 15) to copy.
2. Select **F**ile menu . . . . Alt , F
3. Select **C**opy C
4. Specify new filename . . . . **filename.ext**
5. Select **OK** . . . . ↵

OR **OR**

FROM DOS PROMPT

- ***To copy a file, and place the copy in the same directory as the original file:***

1. Type **COPY** . . . . C O P Y
2. Press **Space** . . . . SPACE
3. Specify filename to copy . . . . . **filename.ext**
4. Press **Space** . . . . SPACE
5. Specify new filename . . . . **filename.ext**
6. **Enter** . . . . ↵

   Example: `COPY NYMETS.TXT NYYANKS.TXT`
   Copies the exact contents of NYMETS.TXT to NYYANKS.TXT.

Continued ...

FROM MS-DOS SHELL

■ ***To copy a file to a specific drive and directory:***

FROM FILE LIST AREA:

1. Select file (page 15) to copy.
2. Select **F**ile menu .... Alt, F
3. Select **C**opy C
4. Specify drive and directory to receive file ...... **drv** : **\path**

   Example: C:\WPDOC
5. Select **OK** .... ↵

OR **OR**

FROM DOS PROMPT

■ ***To copy a file to a specific drive and directory:***

1. Type **COPY** .... C O P Y
2. Press **Space** .... SPACE
3. Specify filename to copy ..... **filename.ext**
4. Press **Space** .... SPACE
5. Specify drive and directory to receive file ...... **drv** : **\path**
6. **Enter** .... ↵

   Example: COPY NYMETS.TXT C:\NATIONAL
   Copies NYMETS.TXT of the current directory to the NATIONAL directory on drive C. The copy will have the same name.

Continued ...

FROM MS-DOS SHELL

To copy selected files to a specific drive and directory:

FROM FILE LIST AREA:

1. Select files (page 15) to copy.
2. Select **F**ile menu . . . . Alt, F
3. Select **C**opy C
4. Specify drive and directory to receive files . . . . . **drv** : **\path**

   Example: C:\WPDOC
5. Select **OK** . . . . ↵

OR **OR**

FROM DOS PROMPT

To copy selected files to a specific drive and directory:

1. Type **COPY** . . . . C O P Y
2. Press **Space** . . . . SPACE
3. Specify files to copy . . . . **filespec**
4. Press **Space** . . . . SPACE
5. Specify drive and directory to receive files . . . . . **drv** : **\path**
6. **Enter** . . . . ↵

   Example: COPY *.* C:\NATIONAL

   Copies all the files from the current directory to the NATIONAL directory on drive C. The copied files will have the same names as the originals.

Continued ...

Example: `COPY *.TXT C:\NATIONAL`
Copies all files with a TXT extension from the current directory to the NATIONAL directory on drive C. The copied files will have the same names as the originals.

DATE

Displays or changes the computer's date.

FROM DOS PROMPT

▪ *To reset the date:*

1. Type **DATE** . . . . D A T E
2. **Enter** . . . . ↵
3. Specify new date as month-day-year . . . . . mm - dd - yy
4. **Enter** . . . . ↵

FROM DOS PROMPT

▪ *To display the date:*

1. Type **DATE** . . . . D A T E
2. **Enter** . . . . ↵
3. **Enter** . . . . ↵

DEL (Erase)

Deletes specified files from disk or diskette.

FROM MS-DOS SHELL

To erase one file:

FROM DIRECTORY TREE AREA:

1. Select directory (page 10) containing file to delete.
2. Select file (page 15) to delete.
3. Select **F**ile menu . . . . Alt, F
4. Select **D**elete . . . . D
5. Select **Yes** . . . . ↵

OR **OR**

FROM DOS PROMPT

To erase one file:

1. Type **DEL** . . . . D E L
2. Press **Space** . . . . SPACE

   If necessary, specify drive and directory containing file to delete . . . . **drv** : **\path**
3. Specify filename to delete . . . . **filename.ext**
4. **Enter** . . . . ↵

   Example: `DEL MYFILE.TXT` *or*
   `DEL B:\DOC\MYFILE.TXT`
   Deletes MYFILE.TXT from the current or specified drive and directory.

Continued ...

FROM MS-DOS SHELL

To erase more than one file:

FROM DIRECTORY TREE AREA:

1. Select directory (page 10) containing files to delete.
2. Select files (page 15) to delete.
3. Select **F**ile menu .... Alt, F
4. Select **D**elete .... D
5. Select **OK** .... ↵
6. Select **Yes** .... ↵
   (for each file to delete)

OR **OR**

FROM DOS PROMPT

To erase more than one file:

1. Type **DEL** .... D E L
2. Press **Space** .... SPACE

   If necessary, specify drive and directory containing file to delete .... **drv** : **\path**
3. Specify files to delete .... **filespec**
4. **Enter** .... ↵

   Example: DEL *.BAK *or*
   DEL B:\DOC*.BAK

   Deletes all files with a BAK extension from the current or specified drive and directory.

Continued ...

FROM MS-DOS SHELL

■ ***To erase all files in the current directory:***

FROM FILE LIST AREA:

1. Select **F**ile menu .... Alt, F
2. Select **S**elect All .... S
3. Press **Del** .... Del
4. Select **OK** .... ↵
5. Select **Yes** .... ↵
   (for each file to delete)

OR **OR**

FROM DOS PROMPT

■ ***To erase all files in the current directory:***

1. Type **DEL** .... D E L
2. Press **Space** .... SPACE
3. Type ***.*** .... * . *
4. **Enter** .... ↵
5. Press **Y** .... Y
   (to delete all files)

   OR **OR**

   Press **N** .... N
   (to cancel deletion)
6. **Enter** .... ↵

   Example: <u>`DEL`</u> <u>`*.*`</u>

Continued ...

Switches for DEL command:

Switches (shown in bold) provide optional information that directs command to act in a specific way.

/p prompts for confirmation before deleting the specified file

Command structure for DEL command:

DEL drv:\path\FILENAME.EXT **/p**

Example: `DEL *.BAK /p`
Deletes all files with BAK extensions and prompts for confirmation before deleting each BAK file.

DIR

Displays a list of files and subdirectories.

FROM MS-DOS SHELL

▩ *To list all files and subdirectories in the current directory:*

FROM DIRECTORY TREE OR FILE LIST AREA:

By default MS-DOS Shell displays all files in the current directory in the File List area.

To view subdirectories of the current directory:

- Press **+** (plus sign) . . . . 

For related information:
See Expanding/Collapsing View of Subdirectories, page 11.
See Changing the File List Display, pages 13,14.
See Showing Expanded Information About a Selected File, Drive, and Directory, page 18.

OR **OR**

Continued ...

FROM DOS PROMPT

- ***To list all files and subdirectories in the current directory:***

1. Type **DIR** .... D I R
2. **Enter** .... ↵

FROM MS-DOS SHELL

- ***To list selected files in the current directory:***

FROM DIRECTORY TREE OR FILE LIST AREA:

1. Select **O**ptions menu .... Alt, O
2. Select **F**ile Display Options .... F
3. Specify files to list .... **filespec**
4. Select **OK** .... ↵

For more information:
See Changing the File List Display, page 13.
See Showing Expanded Information About a Selected File, Drive, and Directory, page 18.

OR **OR**

FROM DOS PROMPT

- ***To list selected files in the current directory:***

1. Type **DIR** .... D I R
2. Press **Space** .... SPACE
3. Specify files to list .... **filespec**
4. **Enter** .... ↵

Continued ...

To list selected files in the current directory (continued):

Example: `DIR *.BAK`
Displays all files with a BAK extension in the current directory.

FROM DOS PROMPT

■ *To redirect list of files to a printer or file:*

1. Type **DIR** .... D I R
2. Press **Space** .... SPACE
3. Specify files to list .... **filespec**
4. Press **Space** .... SPACE
5. Type > (greater-than) .... >
6. Type **PRN** (print device) ...... P R N
   (to redirect output to printer)

   OR **OR**

   Specify a filename .... **filename.ext**
   (to redirect output to a file)
7. **Enter** .... ↵

   Example: `DIR B:\*.BAK >PRN`
   Redirects display of all files with a BAK extension in the root directory of the B drive to the printer.

   Example: `DIR *.BAK >BAKFILE.LST`
   Redirects display of all files with a BAK extension in current directory to BAKFILE.LST file.

   Example: `DIR *.BK! >>BAKFILE.LST`
   *Redirects display of all files with a BK! extension and **appends** list to BAKFILE.LST file.*

Continued ...

Switches for DIR command:

Switches (shown in bold) provide optional information that directs command to act in a specific way.

/p	pauses between screens
/w	list files in a wide format
/s	displays files in current directory and all subdirectories of current directory
/a:attrib	displays only files and subdirectories with the following specified attributes:
	h hidden files
	-h files that are not hidden
	s system files
	-s non system files
	d directories only
	-d files only
	a files to be archived (backed up)
	-a files that have not changed since last backup
	r read-only files
	-r files that are not read-only

Example: `DIR c:\wpdoc\*.frm /p`
Displays all files in WPDOC directory with a FRM extension and pauses between screen displays.

Example: `DIR \ /a:s /s`
Displays all system files in the root directory (\) and all its subdirectories.

Continued ...

Switches (continued)

/o:order displays files and subdirectories in the following sort order:

- n by name
- -n reverse order by name (Z-A)
- e by extension
- -e reverse order by extension (Z-A)
- d by date and time
- -d reverse order by date and time (Last-First)
- s by size
- -s reverse order by size (Largest-Smallest)
- g with directories listed above files
- -g with directories listed below files

Command structure for DIR command:

DIR drv:\path\filespec **a/: /o: /p /w /s**

Example: `DIR /o:e`
Displays all files by extension order.

Example: `DIR /o:-s /o-g`
Displays all files by reverse size order with directories listed below files.

DISKCOPY

Copies the contents of one diskette to another.

NOTE: Diskettes must be of the same size and capacity.

FROM MS-DOS SHELL

■ ***To copy a diskette in drive A to a diskette in drive B:***

FROM PROGRAM LIST AREA — MAIN GROUP:

USING THE KEYBOARD

1. • Press **D** (Disk Utilities) . . . . D
   • **Enter** . . . . ↵
   • Press **D** (Diskcopy) . . . . D
   • **Enter** . . . . ↵

OR **USING A MOUSE** **OR**

1. • Double-click on Disk Utilities.
   • Double-click on Diskcopy.

FROM "DISK COPY" DIALOG BOX:

2. Select **OK** . . . . ↵
   (to accept parameters: a: b:)

3. • Insert source diskette in drive A.
   • Insert target diskette in drive B.
   • Close both drive doors.

4. **Enter** . . . . ↵

Continued ...

To copy a diskette in drive A to a diskette in drive B: (continued):

5. When prompted to Copy another diskette (Y/N)?, Press **Y** .... Y
   (repeat steps 2 & 3)

   OR **OR**

   Press **N** .... N
   (to exit diskcopy)

6. **Enter** .... ↵
   (to return to DOSSHELL)

OR **OR**

FROM DOS PROMPT

To copy a diskette in drive A to a diskette in drive B:

1. Type
   DISKCOPY .. D I S K C O P Y
2. Press **Space** .... SPACE
3. Type **A:** .... A :
4. Press **Space** .... SPACE
5. Type **B:** .... B :

   Example: `DISKCOPY A: B:`
6. **Enter** .... ↵
7. • Insert source diskette in drive A.
   • Insert target diskette in drive B.
   • Close both drive doors.

Continued ...

To copy a diskette in drive A to a diskette in drive B (continued):

8. **Enter** .... ↵
   (to begin copying)

9. When prompted to Copy another diskette (Y/N)?,
   Press **Y** .... Y
   (repeat steps 7 & 8)

   OR **OR**

   Press **N** .... N
   (to exit diskcopy)

10. **Enter** .... ↵

Continued ...

FROM MS-DOS SHELL

To copy a diskette using only one drive:

FROM PROGRAM LIST AREA — MAIN GROUP:

USING THE KEYBOARD

1. • Press **D** (Disk Utilities) .... D
   • **Enter** .... ↵
   • Press **D** (Diskcopy) .... D
   • **Enter** .... ↵

OR **USING A MOUSE** **OR**

1. • Double-click on Disk Utilities.
   • Double-click on Diskcopy.

FROM "DISK COPY" DIALOG BOX:

2. Specify source disk drive .... **drv** :
3. Press **Space** .... SPACE
4. Specify target disk drive .... **drv** :
   Example (steps 2-4) <u>A:</u> <u>A:</u> *or* <u>B:</u> <u>B:</u>
5. Select **OK** .... ↵
6. Insert source diskette in source drive and close drive door.
7. **Enter** .... ↵
   (to begin copying)
8. When prompted to insert target diskette in target drive, remove source diskette and insert target diskette.
9. **Enter** .... ↵
   NOTE: Steps 6-9 may have to be repeated one or more times.

Continued ...

To copy a diskette using only one drive (continued):

10. When prompted to Copy another diskette (Y/N)?,
    Press **Y** .... Y
    (to copy another diskette)

    OR **OR**

    Press **N** .... N
    (to exit diskcopy)

11. **Enter** .... ↵
    (to return to DOSSHELL)

OR **OR**

FROM DOS PROMPT

To copy a diskette using only one drive:

1. Type
   DISKCOPY . . D I S K C O P Y
2. Press **Space** .... SPACE
3. Specify source disk drive .... **drv** :
4. Press **Space** .... SPACE
5. Specify target disk drive .... **drv** :

   Example: DISKCOPY A: A: *or*
   DISKCOPY B: B:
6. **Enter** .... ↵
7. Insert source diskette in source drive and close door.
8. **Enter** .... ↵

Continued ...

To copy a diskette using only one drive (continued):

9. When prompted to insert target diskette in target drive, remove source diskette and insert target diskette.

10. **Enter** .... [↵]

    NOTE: Steps 7-10 may have to be repeated one or more times.

11. When prompted to Copy another diskette (Y/N)?,
    Press **Y** .... [Y]
    (to copy another diskette)

    OR **OR**

    Press **N** .... [N]
    (to exit diskcopy)

12. **Enter** .... [↵]

Switches for DISKCOPY command:

Switches (shown in bold) provide optional information that directs command to act in a specific way.

/1	copies the first side of a disk
/v	verifies that the copy is done correctly

Command structure for DISKCOPY command:

DISKCOPY DRV: DRV: **/1** **/v**

Example: `DISKCOPY a: b: /v`

EDIT

Runs the MS-DOS Editor program. (See APPENDIX — MS-DOS Editor, pages 125,126 for information.)

FROM MS-DOS SHELL

■ *To edit or create an ASCII text file:*

FROM PROGRAM LIST AREA — MAIN GROUP:

USING THE KEYBOARD

1. • Press **E** (Editor) . . . . [E]
   • **Enter** . . . . [↵]

OR **USING A MOUSE** **OR**

1. • Double-click on Editor.

FROM "FILE TO EDIT" DIALOG BOX:

2. Specify drive, directory, and file to edit . . . . . **drv[:]\path\filename**

   Example: c:\batch\wpdoc.bat

3. Select **OK** . . . . [↵]

OR **OR**

FROM DOS PROMPT

■ *To edit or create an ASCII text file:*

1. Type **EDIT** . . . . [E][D][I][T]
2. Press **Space** . . . . [SPACE]
3. Specify drive, directory, and file to edit . . . . . . **drv[:]\path\filename**
4. **Enter** . . . . [↵]

   Example: EDIT c:\batch\wpdoc.bat

FORMAT

Prepares a new hard drive or floppy diskette for use. Warning! This command will erase the entire contents of a disk.

FROM MS-DOS SHELL

▩ ***To format regular (non-system) diskettes:***

FROM PROGRAM LIST AREA — MAIN GROUP:

USING THE KEYBOARD

1. • Press **D** (Disk Utilities) . . . . [D]
   • **Enter** . . . . [↵]
   • Press **F** (Format) . . . . [F]
   • **Enter** . . . . [↵]

OR **USING A MOUSE** **OR**

1. • Double-click on Disk Utilities.
   • Double-click on Format.

FROM "FORMAT" DIALOG BOX:

2. Specify drive to format . . . . **drv**[:]

   If necessary, specify size of diskette to format . . . . [/][F][:]*n*
   where n = a diskette size below:
   160, **180**, **320**, **360**, **720**, **1.2**, **1.44**, **2.88**

   Example: <u>`A:`</u> *or* <u>`A:/F:360`</u>

3. Select **OK** . . . . [↵]
4. Insert diskette in drive and close door.
5. Select **OK** . . . . [↵]

Continued ...

To format regular (non-system) diskettes (continued):

6. When prompted for Volume label,
   Enter .... ↵
7. When prompted to Format another?,
   Press **Y** (Yes) .... Y

   OR **OR**

   Press **N** (to exit format) .... N
8. **Enter** twice .... ↵, ↵
   (to return to DOSSHELL)

OR **OR**

FROM DOS PROMPT

To format regular (non-system) diskettes:

1. Type **FORMAT** .... F O R M A T
2. Press **Space** .... SPACE
3. Specify drive to format .... **drv** :

   If necessary, specify size of diskette to format .... / F : *n*

   where n = a diskette size below:

   160, 180, 320, 360, 720, 1.2, 1.44, 2.88

   Example: `FORMAT A:` *or* `FORMAT A:/f:360`
4. **Enter** .... ↵
5. Insert diskette in drive and close door.
6. **Enter** .... ↵
7. When prompted for Volume label,
   Enter .... ↵

Continued ...

To format regular (non-system) diskettes (continued):

8. When prompted to Format another?, Press **Y** (Yes) .... Y

   OR **OR**

   Press **N** (to exit format) .... N

9. **Enter** .... ↵

FROM MS-DOS SHELL

▩ *To format system (bootable) diskettes:*

FROM PROGRAM LIST AREA — MAIN GROUP:

USING THE KEYBOARD

1. • Press **D** (Disk Utilities) .... D
   • **Enter** .... ↵
   • Press **F** (Format) .... F
   • **Enter** .... ↵

OR **USING A MOUSE** **OR**

1. • Double-click on Disk Utilities.
   • Double-click on Format.

FROM "FORMAT" DIALOG BOX:

2. Specify drive to format .... **drv** :

   If necessary, specify size of diskette to format .... / F : *n*
   where n = a diskette size below:
   160, **180**, **320**, **360**, **720**, **1.2**, **1.44**, **2.88**

3. Type **/S** .... / S

Continued ...

To format system (bootable) diskettes (continued):

Example: A:/s *or* A:/f:360/s

4. Select **OK** .... ↵
5. Insert diskette in drive and close door.
6. **Enter** .... ↵
7. When prompted for Volume label, **Enter** .... ↵
8. When prompted to Format another?, Press **Y** (Yes) .... Y

   OR **OR**

   Press **N** (to exit format) .... N
9. **Enter** twice .... ↵, ↵ (to return to DOSSHELL)

OR **OR**

FROM DOS PROMPT

To format system (bootable) diskettes:

1. Type **FORMAT** .... F O R M A T
2. Press **Space** .... SPACE
3. Specify drive to format .... **drv** :

   If necessary, specify size of diskette to format .... / F : *n*
   where n = a diskette size below:
   160, **180**, **320**, **360**, **720**, **1.2**, **1.44**, **2.88**
4. Type /**S** .... / S

   Example: FORMAT a:/s *or* FORMAT a:/f:720/s
5. **Enter** .... ↵

Continued ...

To format system (bootable) diskettes (continued):

6. Insert diskette in drive and close door.
7. **Enter** .... [↵]
8. When prompted for Volume label,
   Enter .... [↵]
9. When prompted to Format another?,
   Press **Y** (Yes) .... [Y]

   OR **OR**

   Press **N** (to exit format) .... [N]
10. **Enter** .... [↵]

Switches for FORMAT command:

Switches (shown in bold) provide optional information that directs command to act in a specific way.

/v:<u>label</u>	specifies the volume label
/f:<u>size</u>	specifies the size of the diskette to format; use one of the following for the <u>size</u> parameter: <u>160</u>, <u>180</u>, <u>320</u>, <u>360</u>, <u>720</u>, <u>1.2</u>, <u>1.44</u>, <u>2.88</u>
/s	specifies to format the diskette as bootable
/q	specifies that a previously formatted disk be formatted quickly — without scanning for surface errors
/u	specifies that disk be formatted unconditionally — all data is destroyed and disk surface is tested during format

Command structure for FORMAT command:

FORMAT DRV: **/v: /f: /s /q /u**

Example: `FORMAT B: /f:720 /q`
Performs quick format of diskette in drive B: and specifies disk size and type (720K DD, DS).

HELP

Provides online information about DOS commands.

FROM MS-DOS SHELL

■ ***To receive help about a particular command:***

FROM ANY AREA:

1. Select command that you want help on.
2. Press **F1** .... [F1]
   (A help window will appear.)
3. Select **Close** .... [Tab], [↵]
   (to return to DOSSHELL)

OR **OR**

FROM DOS PROMPT

■ ***To receive help about a particular command:***

1. Type **HELP** .... [H][E][L][P]
2. Press **Space** .... [SPACE]
3. Specify DOS command . . . **command name**
4. **Enter** .... [↵]

   Example: `HELP FORMAT`
   Displays help information about the FORMAT command.

MEM

Displays the amount of available and used memory.

FROM DOS PROMPT

■ ***To display memory information:***

1. Type **MEM** .... M E M
2. **Enter** .... ↵

Switches for MEM command:

Switches (shown in bold) provide optional information that directs command to act in a specific way.

/p shows programs currently loaded in memory.

/d shows program and device drivers currently loaded in conventional and upper memory.

/c shows additional information about programs listed in conventional and upper memory.

Command structure for MEM command:

MEM **/p /d /c**

MIRROR

Starts the Mirror program that keeps track of deleted files on a specified disk (deletion-tracking).

FROM DOS PROMPT

- ***To save a copy of a drive's file allocation table and root directory and to install deletion-tracking:***

1. Type **MIRROR** .... M I R R O R
2. Press **Space** .... SPACE
3. Type **/T** .... / T
4. Specify drive letter .... **drv**
5. **Enter** .... ↵

Example: <u>`MIRROR`</u> <u>`/TC`</u>

The following messages will be displayed:

```
Drive C being processed.
The MIRROR process was successful.
Deletion-tracking software being
installed.

The following drives are supported:
Drive C-Default files saved.

Installation complete.
```

Continued ...

FROM DOS PROMPT

■ *To save a copy of the partition table of your hard disk:*

1. Type **MIRROR** .... M I R R O R
2. Press **Space** .... SPACE
3. Type **/PARTN** ..... / P A R T N
4. **Enter** .... ↵
5. Insert diskette.
6. Specify diskette drive letter .... **drv**
7. **Enter** .... ↵

   Example: MIRROR /PARTN
   This command will save the PARTNSAV.FIL file on the specified drive to be used with the UNFORMAT command.

FROM DOS PROMPT

■ *To remove deletion-tracking:*

1. Type **MIRROR** .... M I R R O R
2. Press **Space** .... SPACE
3. Type **/U** .... / U
4. **Enter** .... ↵

   Example: MIRROR /U

Continued ...

Switches for MIRROR command:

Switches (shown in bold) provide optional information that directs command to act in a specific way.

/ldrv	saves only latest disk information for specified drive letter
/partn	saves information about the hard disk partition table to a specified drive (drv:). This information can be used by the RESTORE command to rebuild a damaged or lost partition table
/tdrv-#	loads deletion-tracking program for specified drive letter. You may specify maximum number (-#) of entries in deletion-tracking file
/u	unloads deletion tracking

Command structure for MIRROR command:

MIRROR drv: **/l**drv **/t**drv **/u** **/partn**

Example: `MIRROR /partn`
Saves information about the hard disk partition table to a file.

Example: `MIRROR /tc-25`
Loads deletion-tracking program and specifies 25 as the maximum number of entries to keep in deletion-tracking file.

MKDIR (MD)

Make a new directory.

FROM MS-DOS SHELL

■ ***To create a new subdirectory in the current directory:***

NOTE: To create a first-level subdirectory highlight the root directory (C:\) before executing steps below.

FROM DIRECTORY TREE AREA:

1. Select **F**ile menu . . . . Alt, F
2. Select **C**reate Directory C
3. Specify new directory name. **directory name**
4. Select **OK** . . . . ↵

OR **OR**

FROM DOS PROMPT

■ ***To create a new subdirectory in the current directory:***

1. Type **MD** . . . . M D
2. Press **Space** . . . . SPACE
3. Specify new directory name . . . **directory name**
4. **Enter** . . . . ↵

   Example: MD GL
   If C:\ACCT is the current directory, this will create the subdirectory C:\ACCT\GL.

   NOTE: The new directory cannot have the same name as an existing subdirectory in the current directory.

MODE

Configures (sets up) system devices such as serial ports and printers.

FROM DOS PROMPT

▪ *To configure a printer connected to a parallel port:*

1. Type **MODE** . . . . M O D E
2. Press **Space** . . . . SPACE
3. Type **LPT*n*** . . . . L P T *n*
   (where n = parallel port # 1-3)
4. Press **:** (colon) . . . . :
5. Specify number of columns . . . . **number**
6. Press **,** (comma) . . . . ,
7. Specify number of lines/inch . . . . . . **number**
8. Press **,** (comma) . . . . ,
9. Specify retry action . . . . **letter**
   - **e** return an error if port is busy
   - **b** return "busy" if port is busy
   - **n** do not try to retry if port is busy
   - **p** continue to retry if port is busy
   - **r** return "ready" if port is busy
10. **Enter** . . . . ↵

    Example: `MODE LPT1:80,6,P`
    Sets parallel port 1 to print 80 columns, 6 lines/inch, and to continue to retry if port is busy.

Continued ...

FROM DOS PROMPT

▪ *To configure a serial port:*

1. Type **MODE** .... M O D E
2. Press **Space** .... SPACE
3. Type **COM*n*** .... C O M *n*
   (where n = serial port # 1-4)
4. Press **:** (colon) .... :
5. Specify baud rate .... **number**
   11 = 110 baud **15** = 150 baud **30** = 300 baud
   60 = 600 baud **12** = 1200 baud **24** = 2400 baud
   48 = 4800 baud **96** = 9600 baud **19** = 19,200 baud
6. Press **,** (comma) .... ,
7. Specify parity .... **letter**
   E = even **M** = mark **N** = none **O** = odd
8. Press **,** (comma) .... ,
9. Specify data bits (5-8) .... **number**
10. Press **,** (comma) .... ,
11. Specify stop bits .... **number**
    (1 or 1.5 or 2)
12. Press **,** (comma) .... ,
13. Specify retry action .... **letter**
    - **e** return an error message if port is busy
    - **b** return "busy" if port is busy
    - **n** do not retry if port is busy
    - **p** continue to retry if port is busy
    - **r** return "ready" if port is busy
14. **Enter** .... ↵
    Example: `MODE COM1:96,N,8,1,p`
    Sets COM port 1 to 9600 baud, no parity, 8 data bits, 1 stop bit, and to continue retrying until printer accepts output.

Continued ...

FROM DOS PROMPT

▪ *To redirect printing from a parallel port to a serial port:*

1. Type **MODE** . . . . M O D E
2. Press **Space** . . . . SPACE
3. Type **LPT*n*** . . . . L P T *n*
   (where n = parallel port # 1-3)
4. Press = (equal sign) . . . . =
5. Type **COM*n*** . . . . C O M *n*
   (where n = serial port # 1-4)
6. **Enter** . . . . ↵

   Example: `MODE LPT1=COM1`
   Redirects output directed to LPT1 to COM1.

   NOTE: If this command is issued, be sure to configure COM1.
   See Configure a Serial Port, page 88.

FROM DOS PROMPT

▪ *To cancel printing redirection:*

1. Type **MODE** . . . . M O D E
2. Press **Space** . . . . SPACE
3. Type **LPT*n*** . . . . L P T *n*
   (where n = parallel port # 1-3)
4. **Enter** . . . . ↵

   Example: `MODE LPT1`
   If output was redirected from LPT1 to COM1, this command will cancel redirection and allow output to return to LPT1.

PATH

Sets a search path for executable (.exe), batch (.bat), and command (.com) files. It is used to inform DOS which directories to search if it does not find the command in the current directory.

FROM DOS PROMPT

■ ***To create a search path list:***

1. Type **PATH** . . . . [P][A][T][H]
2. Press **Space** . . . . [SPACE]
3. Specify drive, and directory to include in search path . . . . **drv**[:]**\path**
4. Press ; (semicolon) . . . . [;]
5. Repeat steps 3 and 4 to include additional search directories.
6. **Enter** . . . . [↵]

   Example:
   `PATH C:\DOS;C:\PARADOX3;C:\BATCH`
   Enables the execution of executable, batch, and command files in the DOS, PARADOX3, and BATCH directories from any directory.

   NOTE: This command is usually issued in the AUTOEXEC.BAT file. *See APPENDIX — About autoexec.bat, page 128.*

Continued ...

FROM DOS PROMPT

■ ***To display the current path search setting:***

1. Type **PATH** . . . . [P] [A] [T] [H]
2. **Enter** . . . . [↵]

FROM DOS PROMPT

■ ***To clear the path search settings:***

1. Type **PATH** . . . . [P] [A] [T] [H]
2. Press **Space** . . . . [SPACE]
3. Press **;** (semicolon) . . . . [;]
4. **Enter** . . . . [↵]

   Example: `PATH ;`

PRINT

Prints text files.

FROM MS-DOS SHELL

▪ *To print one or more text files:*

NOTE: You must run Print.com (page 93) from the DOS prompt (before starting MS-DOS Shell) to use this feature.

FROM FILE LIST AREA:

1. Select file(s) (page 15) to print.
2. Select **F**ile menu . . . . Alt, F
3. Select **P**rint . . . . P

OR **OR**

FROM DOS PROMPT

▪ *To print one or more text files:*

1. Type **PRINT** . . . . P R I N T
2. Press **Space** . . . . SPACE
3. Specify drive, directory and files to print . . . . **drv** : **\path\filespec**
4. **Enter** . . . . ↵

   NOTE: The first time this command is issued the prompt "Name of list device [PRN]:" will appear. Press ***Enter*** *to continue.*

   Example: `PRINT C:\BATCH\*.BAT`
   This command will print all files with a BAT extension in the BATCH directory on the C drive.

Continued ...

FROM DOS PROMPT

■ *To cancel the printing of one or more files:*

1. Type **PRINT** .... P R I N T
2. Press **Space** .... SPACE
3. Specify file(s) to cancel .... **filespec**
4. Press **Space** .... SPACE
5. Type **/C** .... / C
6. **Enter** .... ↵

   Example: PRINT *.BAT /C
   Cancel all print jobs of files with a BAT extension.

FROM DOS PROMPT

■ *To cancel the printing of all files:*

1. Type **PRINT** .... P R I N T
2. Press **Space** .... SPACE
3. Type **/T** .... / T

   Example: PRINT /T
4. **Enter** .... ↵

   The message "Print queue is empty." *will be displayed.*

FROM DOS PROMPT

■ *To run Print.com or to view files that are waiting to be printed:*

1. Type **PRINT** .... P R I N T
2. **Enter** .... ↵

PROMPT

To customize the DOS prompt (>).

FROM DOS PROMPT

▩ *To customize the DOS prompt to display the current drive and path:*

1. Type **PROMPT** .... P R O M P T
2. Press **Space** .... SPACE
3. Type **PG** .... $ P $ G
4. **Enter** .... ↵

   Example: PROMPT PG
   If the current directory is \ACT\GL on the C drive, the DOS prompt will appear as: `C:\ACT\GL>`

   NOTE: This command is usually issued in the AUTOEXEC.BAT file. *See APPENDIX — About autoexec.bat, page 128.*

Switch for PROMPT command:

Switch (shown in bold) provides optional information that directs command to act in a specific way.

Text Specifies text to display in system prompt. The following special characters can be added to show additional information in the system prompt:

$B	displays |
$D	displays current date
$G	displays >
$L	displays <
$P	displays current drive and path
$T	displays current time
$V	displays DOS version number

Command structure for PROMPT command:

PROMPT **text**

Example: `PROMPT Today is: $D`
Changes prompt to: `Today is: Sat 08-24-91_`

RENAME (REN)

Renames a file.

FROM MS-DOS SHELL

■ ***To rename a file:***

FROM FILE LIST AREA:

1. Select file (page 15) to rename.
2. Select **F**ile menu . . . . Alt, F
3. Select Re**n**ame . . . . N
4. Specify new filename . . . . **filename.ext**

   Example: NEWNAME.TXT
5. Select **OK** . . . . ↵

OR **OR**

FROM DOS PROMPT

■ ***To rename a file:***

1. Type **REN** . . . . R E N
2. Press **Space** . . . . SPACE
3. Specify file to rename . . . . **filename.ext**
4. Press **Space** . . . . SPACE
5. Specify new filename . . . . **filename.ext**
6. **Enter** . . . . ↵

   Example: REN APRIL.TXT MAY.TXT
   Renames APRIL.TXT to MAY.TXT.

Continued ...

FROM MS-DOS SHELL

▩ *To rename a directory:*

NOTE: Renaming a directory can only be accomplished through the DOSSHELL.

FROM DIRECTORY TREE AREA:

1. Select directory (page 10) to rename.
2. Select **F**ile menu .... Alt, F
3. Select Re**n**ame .... N

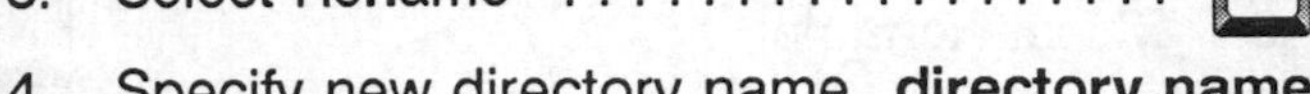

4. Specify new directory name. **directory name**
5. Select **OK** .... ↵

RESTORE

Restores backed-up files.

FROM MS-DOS SHELL

To restore all files from a set of backup diskettes to a hard disk:

FROM PROGRAM LIST AREA — MAIN GROUP:

USING THE KEYBOARD

1. • Press **D** (Disk Utilities) . . . . D
   • **Enter** . . . . ↵
   • Press **R** (Restore Fixed Disk) . . . . . . R
   • **Enter** . . . . ↵

OR **USING A MOUSE** **OR**

1. • Double-click on Disk Utilities.
   • Double-click on Restore Fixed Disk.

FROM "RESTORE FIXED DISK" DIALOG BOX:

2. Specify source drive . . . . **drv** :
3. Press **Space** . . . . SPACE
4. Specify destination drive . . . . **drv** :
5. Type ***.*/S** . . . . \ * . * / S

   Example (steps 2-5): <u>`A:`</u> <u>`C:\*.*/S`</u>
6. Select **OK** . . . . ↵
7. Insert backup diskette when prompted.
8. Press **Space** . . . . SPACE
9. Repeat steps 6 and 7 if prompted.
10. **Enter** (to return to DOSSHELL) . . . . . . ↵

Continued...

OR **OR**

FROM DOS PROMPT

■ ***To restore all files from a set of backup diskettes to a hard disk:***

1. Type **RESTORE.** R E S T O R E
2. Press **Space** . . . . SPACE
3. Type **A:** . . . . A :

   OR **OR**

   Type **B:** . . . . B :
4. Press **Space** . . . . SPACE
5. Specify destination drive . . . . **drv** :
6. Type *.* . . . . \ * . *
7. Press **Space** . . . . SPACE
8. Type /**S** . . . . / S
   (to restore all subdirectories)
9. **Enter** . . . . ↵
10. Insert backup diskette when prompted.
11. Press **Space** . . . . SPACE
12. Repeat steps 10 and 11 if prompted to insert another diskette.

    Example: RESTORE A: C:*.* /S

    NOTE: *You cannot restore files to a directory that does not exist. To successfully restore the files, create the directory first. See MKDIR, page 86.*

Continued ...

FROM MS-DOS SHELL

▪ *To restore selected files from a set of backup diskettes to a hard disk:*

FROM PROGRAM LIST AREA — MAIN GROUP:

USING THE KEYBOARD

1. • Press **D** (Disk Utilities) . . . . [D]
   • **Enter** . . . . [↵]
   • Press **R** (Restore Fixed Disk) . . . . . . [R]
   • **Enter** . . . . [↵]

OR USING A MOUSE OR

1. • Double-click on Disk Utilities.
   • Double-click on Restore Fixed Disk.

FROM "RESTORE FIXED DISK" DIALOG BOX:

2. Specify source drive . . . . **drv** [:]
3. Press **Space** . . . . [SPACE]
4. Specify destination drlve . . . .**drv** [:]
5. Specify directory and files to restore. . . . . **\path\filespec**
6. Select **OK** . . . . [↵]
7. Insert backup diskette when prompted.
8. Press **Space** . . . . [SPACE]
9. Repeat steps 7 and 8 if prompted to insert another diskette.
10. **Enter** . . . . [↵]
    (to return to DOSSHELL)

Continued ...

OR **OR**

FROM DOS PROMPT

▪ *To restore selected files from a set of backup diskettes to a hard disk:*

1. Type **RESTORE**. R E S T O R E
2. Press **Space** .... SPACE
3. Type **A:** .... A :

   OR **OR**

   Type **B:** .... B :
4. Press **Space** .... SPACE
5. Specify destination drive, directory, and files to restore. .... **drv** : **\path\filespec**
6. **Enter** .... ↵
7. Insert backup disk when prompted.
8. Press **Space** .... SPACE
9. Repeat steps 7 and 8 if prompted to insert another diskette.

   Example: RESTORE A: C:\ACCT\GL*.DAT
   This will only restore the backed-up files with a DAT extension from the C:\ACCT\GL directory.

   NOTE: You cannot restore files to any directory other than the directory from which they were backed up.

Continued ...

Switches for RESTORE Command:

Switches (shown in bold) provide optional information that directs command to act in a specific way.

/s restores all subdirectories

/p prompts for permission to restore files that are read-only or files that have changed since the last backup

/b:date restores only files modified on or before the specified date. (Enter date as mm-yy-dd.)

/a:date restores only files modified on or after the specified date. (Enter date as mm-yy-dd.)

/d displays files that match filespec without restoring files

Command structure for RESTORE command:

RESTORE DRV: DRV:\path\filespec **/s /p /b: /a: /d**

Example: `RESTORE A: C:\pies\*.* /d`
Displays all files on backup disk in PIES directory.

Example: `RESTORE DRV: DRV:\*.* /a:08-20-91`
Restores only files modified on or after 08-20-91.

RMDIR (RD)

Removes an empty directory.

FROM MS-DOS SHELL

■ *To remove an empty directory:*

FROM DIRECTORY TREE AREA:

1. Select directory (page 10) to remove.
2. Select **F**ile menu .... Alt, F
3. Select **D**elete .... D
4. Select **Yes** .... ↵

OR **OR**

FROM DOS PROMPT

■ *To remove an empty directory:*

1. Type **RD** .... R D
2. Press **Space** .... SPACE
3. Specify directory name .... **directory name**
4. **Enter** .... ↵

   Example: RD GL
   If the current directory is \ACCT, this command will remove the GL directory, providing it is empty.

   NOTE: Use the DELETE command to erase files from the directory before removing it. (See DEL, page 63 to erase all files in the current directory.)

SUBST

Associates a path with a logical drive letter.

FROM DOS PROMPT

■ *To associate a path with a logical drive letter:*

1. Type **SUBST** . . . . S U B S T
2. Press **Space** . . . . SPACE
3. Specify logical drive . . . . **drv** :

   NOTE: Do not use the drive letter of an existing physical drive.

4. Press **Space** . . . . SPACE
5. Specify drive and directory . . . **drv** : **\path**
6. **Enter** . . . . ↵

   Example: SUBST Z: C:\ACCT\GL
   This command will associate the directory C:\ACCT\GL with logical drive Z. Whenever you want to change to the GL directory, all you have to do is type Z: and press enter to reach that directory.

FROM DOS PROMPT

■ *To cancel a path associated with a logical drive:*

1. Type **SUBST** . . . . S U B S T
2. Press **Space** . . . . SPACE
3. Type **/D** . . . . / D
4. **Enter** . . . . ↵

   Example: SUBST /D

TIME

Sets or displays the system time.

FROM DOS PROMPT

▩ *To set the system time:*

1. Type **TIME** . . . . T I M E
2. Press **Space** . . . . SPACE
3. Specify new time as hours:minutes . . . . **hh** : **mm**
4. **Enter** . . . . ↵

   Example: TIME 13:00
   This will set the system time to 1:00 P.M. The computer uses military time.

FROM DOS PROMPT

▩ *To display the system time:*

1. Type **TIME** . . . . T I M E
2. **Enter** . . . . ↵
3. **Enter** . . . . ↵

TYPE

Displays an ASCII (unformatted) text file.

FROM MS-DOS SHELL

▩ *To display contents of a text file:*

FROM FILE LIST AREA:

1. Select file (page 15) to display.
2. Select **F**ile menu . . . . Alt, F
3. Select **V**iew File Contents V
4. Select **OK** . . . . ↵
   (to end viewing)

OR **OR**

FROM DOS PROMPT

▩ *To display contents of a text file:*

1. Type **TYPE** . . . . T Y P E
2. Press **Space** . . . . SPACE
3. Specify filename . . . . **filename.ext**
4. **Enter** . . . . ↵

   Example: TYPE AUTOEXEC.BAT

   NOTE: *If the specified file is not an ASCII text file, strange characters will be displayed and the computer may beep. Do not get alarmed, the computer is merely displaying non-text code.*

Continued ...

FROM DOS PROMPT

■ ***To redirect display of contents of a text file to a printer:***

1. Type **TYPE** .... T Y P E
2. Press **Space** .... SPACE
3. Specify filename .... **filename.ext**
4. Type > (greater-than) .... >
5. Type **PRN** (print device) ...... P R N
   (to redirect output to printer)
6. **Enter** .... ↵

   Example: `TYPE MENU.DAT>PRN`
   Redirects display of MENU.DAT file in current directory to the printer.

UNDELETE

Restores deleted files.

CAUTION! Once a file is deleted, it may not be recoverable if other files have been added or changed since the deletion.

FROM MS-DOS SHELL

■ ***To list files that are available to be recovered:***

FROM DIRECTORY TREE AREA:

1. Select directory (page 10) where files existed.
2. Select Program List area (page 6).

FROM PROGRAM LIST AREA — MAIN GROUP:

USING THE KEYBOARD

3. • Press **D** (Disk Utilities) . . . . D
   • **Enter** . . . . ↵
   • Press **U** (Undelete) . . . . U
   • **Enter** . . . . ↵

OR **USING A MOUSE** **OR**

3. • Double-click on Disk Utilities.
   • Double-click on Undelete.

FROM "UNDELETE" DIALOG BOX:

4. Select **OK** . . . . ↵
5. **Enter** . . . . ↵
   (to return to DOSSHELL)

OR **OR**

Continued ...

FROM DOS PROMPT

- ***To list files that are available to be recovered:***

1. Change to the directory where the file existed. (See CD, page 52.)
2. Type **UNDELETE** . . U N D E L E T E
3. Press **Space** . . . . SPACE
4. Type **/LIST** . . . . / L I S T
5. **Enter** . . . . ↵

   Example: <u>`UNDELETE`</u> <u>`/LIST`</u>

Continued ...

FROM MS-DOS SHELL

▪ *To undelete a specific file:*

FROM DIRECTORY TREE AREA:

1. Select directory (page 10) where file existed.
2. Select Program List area (page 6).

FROM PROGRAM LIST AREA — MAIN GROUP:

USING THE KEYBOARD

3. • Press **D** (Disk Utilities) . . . . D
   • **Enter** . . . . ↵
   • Press **U** (Undelete) . . . . U
   • **Enter** . . . . ↵

OR **USING A MOUSE** **OR**

3. • Double-click on Disk Utilities.
   • Double-click on Undelete.

FROM "UNDELETE" DIALOG BOX:

4. Specify filename to restore . . . . **filename.ext**
5. Select **OK** . . . . ↵
6. Press **Y** . . . . Y
7. Press first letter of filename . . . . **letter**
8. **Enter** . . . . ↵

NOTE: Restored file will not reappear in file list until disk is refreshed. (See Updating Display of Disk Information for Current Drive, page 12.)

OR **OR**

Continued ...

FROM DOS PROMPT

▪ ***To undelete a specific file:***

1. Change to the directory where the file existed. (See CD, page 52.)
2. Type **UNDELETE** . . U N D E L E T E
3. Press **Space** . . . . SPACE
4. Specify filename to restore . . . **filename.ext**
5. **Enter** . . . . ↵
6. Press **Y** . . . . Y
7. Press first letter of filename . . . . **letter**
8. **Enter** . . . . ↵

   Example: `UNDELETE AUTOEXEC.BAT`
   This command will recover the AUTOEXEC.BAT file of the current directory as long as it is available.

Continued ...

FROM MS-DOS SHELL

To undelete all files in the current directory without prompting:

FROM PROGRAM LIST AREA — MAIN GROUP:

USING THE KEYBOARD

1. • Press **D** (Disk Utilities) . . . . D
   • **Enter** . . . . ↵
   • Press **U** (Undelete) . . . . U
   • **Enter** . . . . ↵

OR **USING A MOUSE** **OR**

1. • Double-click on Disk Utilities.
   • Double-click on Undelete.

FROM "UNDELETE" DIALOG BOX:

2. Type **/ALL** . . . . / A L L
3. Select **OK** . . . . ↵
4. **Enter** . . . . ↵
   (to return to DOSSHELL)

OR **OR**

FROM DOS PROMPT

To undelete all files of the current directory without prompting:

1. Type **UNDELETE** . . U N D E L E T E
2. Press **Space** . . . . SPACE

Continued ...

To undelete all files of the current directory without prompting (continued):

3. Type **/ALL** . . . . [/] [A] [L] [L]
4. **Enter** . . . . [↵]

   Example: `UNDELETE /ALL`

NOTE: *This command will attempt to recover all deleted files in the current directory. If a file that is to be recovered has the same name as an existing file, the first letter of the recovered file will be changed so that the name will be unique.*

Switches for UNDELETE command:

Switches (shown in bold) provide optional information that directs command to act in a specific way.

/list lists deleted files that are available to be recovered.

/all recovers all deleted files without prompting for confirmation.

/dos recovers files that are available internally to DOS, prompting for confirmation of each file. If deletion-tracking is installed, it is ignored.

/dt recovers files listed in the deletion-tracking file, prompting for confirmation of each file. (See MIRROR command, page 83.)

Command structure for UNDELETE command:

UNDELETE drv:\path\filename **/list /all /dos /dt**

Example: `UNDELETE c:\temp\*.* /all`
Recovers all files in TEMP directory on drive C:.

Example: `UNDELETE *.* /lst`
Lists deleted files that can be recovered.

UNFORMAT

Restores a disk changed by the FORMAT command.

FROM DOS PROMPT

■ ***To determine if the C drive can be unformatted by using a mirror file:***

1. Type **UNFORMAT**. U N F O R M A T
2. Press **Space** . . . . SPACE
3. Type **/J** . . . . / J
4. **Enter** . . . . ↵

   Example: <u>UNFORMAT</u> <u>/J</u>

FROM DOS PROMPT

■ ***To unformat a formatted disk:***

1. Type **UNFORMAT**. U N F O R M A T
2. Press **Space** . . . . SPACE
3. Specify drive to restore . . . . **drv** :
4. **Enter** . . . . ↵
5. **Enter** . . . . ↵
6. Press **Y** . . . . Y
7. **Enter** . . . . ↵

   Example: <u>UNFORMAT</u> <u>A:</u>

Continued ...

FROM DOS PROMPT

■ ***To rebuild a damaged partition table of the C drive:***

1. Type **UNFORMAT**. U N F O R M A T
2. Press **Space** .... SPACE
3. Type **/PARTN** ..... / P A R T N
4. Insert the disk containing the PARTNSAV.FIL file created by the MIRROR command (page 83.)
5. Specify drive letter of disk containing the PARTNSAV.FIL file .... **drv**
6. **Enter** .... ↵

   Example: UNFORMAT /PARTN

Switches for UNFORMAT command:

Switches (shown in bold) provide optional information that directs command to act in a specific way.

/j	confirms that file created by MIRROR command exists and that file agrees with system information about disk.
/u	unformats a disk without using file created by MIRROR command
/l	when used without /partn switch, displays every file and subdirectory found by UNFORMAT command. When used with the /partn switch, displays the partition table and information about the current drive
/test	displays information about how UNFORMAT would recreate disk information
/partn	uses PARTNSAV.FIL file (created with MIRROR command) to restore damaged partition table of a hard disk

Continued ...

Command structure for UNFORMAT command:

UNFORMAT drv: **/j /u /l /test /partn**

Example: `UNFORMAT c: /u`
Unformats drive C without using file created by MIRROR command.

VER

Displays DOS version number.

FROM DOS PROMPT

To display DOS version number:

1. Type **VER** . . . . V E R
2. **Enter** . . . . ↵

XCOPY

Copies files and subdirectories of a specified directory.

FROM DOS PROMPT

To copy all files and subdirectories of specified directory:

1. Type **XCOPY** . . . . X C O P Y
2. Press **Space** . . . . SPACE
3. Specify drive and directory . . . **drv** : **\path**
4. Press **Space** . . . . SPACE

Continued ...

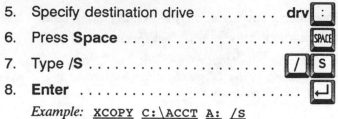

5. Specify destination drive .... **drv** [:]
6. Press **Space** .... [SPACE]
7. Type **/S** .... [/] [S]
8. **Enter** .... [↵]

   Example: XCOPY C:\ACCT A: /S
   Copies all files and subdirectories of the ACCT directory on drive C to drive A.

Switches for XCOPY command:

Switches (shown in bold) provide optional information that directs command to act in a specific way.

/d:date	copies only files modified on or after specified date; enter date as mm-dd-yy.
/e	copies directories and subdirectories, even if they are empty; the /s switch must also be used with this.
/p	prompts for confirmation on whether or not destination files should be created.
/s	copies directories and subdirectories; will not copy empty directories.
/m	copies only files that have been modified or created since last XCOPY command and resets archive file attribute
/a	copies only files that have been modified or created since last XCOPY command and does not reset archive file attribute
/v	verifies that copy is like original file

Command structure for XCOPY command:

XCOPY drv:\path\filespec drv: **/d: /e /p /s /m /a**

Example: XCOPY C:\wpdoc*.frm A: **/m /v**
Copies only files with FRM extensions that have been created or modified since last XCOPY command and verifies copies are accurate.

APPENDIX

KEY COMMANDS

General Purpose Keys

▪ *To interrupt a DOS command:*

- Press [Ctrl]+[C] to cancel the execution of a DOS command.

▪ *To pause the execution of a program:*

- Press [Ctrl]+[S] to suspend a program's execution.

NOTE: *To cancel the pause/freeze effect, press any other key.*

▪ *To print contents of computer screen:*

- Press [PrtSc] or [Shift]+[PrtSc] (Print Screen)

NOTE: *Some computers have a separate Print-Screen key.*

▪ *To switch Caps Lock on and off:*

- Press [Caps Lock] once to switch to all capitals.
- Press [Caps Lock] again to switch back to normal.

▪ *To switch the cursor/number keypad between numbers and cursor mode:*

- Press [Num Lock] (Number Lock) once to switch to cursor mode.
- Press [Num Lock] again to switch back to numbers mode.

Command Line Keys

The following keys are used only at the command line.

To erase the previous character on the command line:

- Press BKSP (Backspace)

To cancel a command entry before completing it:

- Press Esc (Escape)

To repeat the last DOS command entered:

- Press F3

To repeat the last DOS command entered, one character at a time:

- Press F1 repeatedly.

MS-DOS ERROR MESSAGES

The table that follows lists common MS-DOS error messages (in the shaded boxes), the reason(s) errors may occur, and actions to resolve them.

Bad command or filename

Reason: The last entry was not a valid command, or MS-DOS did not find a program of that name in the current drive and directory.

Action:
- Retype command correctly.

or
- Change to the directory (page 52) and/or drive (page 55) that contains program to run, then re-enter command.

or
- Re-enter command, specifying the location of the program to run. (For example, type c:\wp51\wp)

or
- Insert the correct diskette (containing the program to run) in the floppy drive, then re-enter command.

Cannot execute DRV\PATH\PROGNAME.EXT

Reason: Program specified in last command is too large to be loaded in available memory.

Action:
- If possible, exit any applications that may be running (taking up memory space), then try to run application again.

or
- Use the MEM /C command to determine how memory is being used. If necessary, change startup configuration files (edit config.sys and/or autoexec.bat (page 128)), then restart system.

Drive types or diskette types not compatible

Reason: The command used requires drives and diskettes of the same size and density.

Action:
- If possible, change diskettes so that their size and density match, then re-enter command.

or
- If possible, use the same disk drive and alter command (e.g., DISKCOPY A: A:).

or
- Use an alternate command that does not require identical diskette types. (e.g., Use COPY instead of DISKCOPY)

Duplicate filename or file not found

Reason: RENAME command failed because it attempted to rename a file to a filename that already exists, or it failed because the file to be renamed could not be located.

Action:
- Re-enter RENAME command using appropriate filenames. (e.g., type RENAME old.nam unique.nam)

File/Path not found

Reason: MS-DOS could not find specified filename or directory (path) as specified in last command.

Action:
- Re-enter command using correct filename or path (e.g., COPY C:\dirnam\actual.nam B:).

or
- Change to the drive or directory that contains filename, then re-enter command.

General failure reading drive A or B...
Abort, Retry, Fail?

Reason: Diskette in drive A or B has not been formatted or diskette is damaged.

Action:
- Press R to retry.
  If error message is repeated,
  - remove disk and replace with a formatted diskette, then press R.

  If error occurs on a hard disk, call for technical help.

Insert disk with \COMMAND.COM in drive A or B and strike any key when ready

Reason: MS-DOS can't find COMMAND.COM file. (This file must be present in the root directory of the startup drive.)

Action:
- Put the DOS startup disk back into drive A and press any key.

or
- If your system was started from a hard drive, restart system using a MS-DOS 5.0 startup disk in drive A:, then copy COMMAND.COM from startup disk to hard drive's root directory. (e.g., COPY a:\COMMAND.COM C:\)

Insufficient disk space

Reason: File being saved or copied is larger than remaining space on target disk.

Action:
- Use DIR command to check contents of target disk, then (if possible) erase unnecessary files on the disk before re-entering command.

or
- Insert a new formatted disk before re-entering last command.

Invalid drive specification

Reason: Last command included a reference to a drive that does not exist.

Action:
- Re-enter command using a valid drive specification (e.g., DIR B:).

Invalid number of parameters

Reason: Your last command contained too many or too few parameters. "Parameters" are information you typed after a command name.

Action:
- Re-enter command using correct spacing and number of parameters.

Non-system disk or disk error

Reason: The startup disk (drive A or C) does not contain system files.

Action:
- Insert an MS-DOS startup disk in drive A and press any key.

or

- If using a hard disk system, remove non-system disk from drive A and press any key.

Not ready reading/writing drive A or B...
Abort, Retry, Fail?

Reason: Diskette is missing or drive door/latch/button is open.

Action:
- Insert a diskette in specified drive and close drive door, latch or button.

  or
- Make sure drive door, latch or button is closed.
- Press R to Retry.

Sector not found reading drive A or B...

Reason: Diskette in drive A or B has not been formatted or diskette is damaged.

Action:
- Press R to retry.

  If error message is repeated,
  - remove disk and replace with a formatted diskette, then press R.

  If error occurs on a hard disk, call for technical help.

Terminate batch job (Y/N)?	
Reason:	You pressed CTRL+BREAK during the execution of a batch file.
Action:	• Press Y (Yes) or N (No).

Unable to create directory	
Reason:	The last MD or MKDIR command specified a directory name that already exists.
Action:	• Re-enter MD command using a unique directory name or enter a CD command if that was your intention.

Write fault error writing device LPT1, COM1...	
Reason:	Device (printer, modem, etc.) is either not turned on, not connected to computer, not on-line, or cables are not tight.
Action:	• Make sure the connections between device and computer are tight and that device is turned on and on-line. • Press R to Retry.

MS-DOS EDITOR

■ *MS-DOS Editor — Menus and Options:*

Menu	Item	Description
File	New	Clears current file and starts a new untitled file.
	Open	Retrieves a file stored on disk.
	Save As	Saves and renames current file.
	Print	Prints file in memory.
	Exit	Exits Editor program.
Edit	Cut	Removes and transfers selected text to Clipboard.
	Copy	Copies selected text to Clipboard.
	Paste	Inserts transferred text from Clipboard into document.
	Clear	Deletes selected text.
Search	Find	Searches document for specified text.
	Repeat Last Find	Continues search using previous search text.
	Change	Finds and replaces text. Provides for case sensitive and whole word searches. Provides for "verify" and "global replace" modes.
Options	Display	Provides for settings of colors for editor. Provides for setting number of tab stops and for use of scroll bars.
	Help Path	Provides for specifying directory location of Editor Help file.

MS-DOS Editor — Keys:

Cursor Movement Keys:	
ARROWS	Move cursor up, down, left, right, in direction of arrow keys
CTRL+LEFT	Move left one word
CTRL+RIGHT	Move right one word
HOME	Move to first character of current line
END	Move to end of current line
CTRL+ENTER	Move to beginning of next line
Scrolling Keys:	
CTRL+UP/DOWN	Scroll up/down one line
CTRL+LEFT/RIGHT	Scroll left/right one window
PGUP/PGDN	Scroll up/down one screen
CTRL+K,0-3	Set bookmarks (specify 0-3)
CTRL+Q,0-3	Go to specified bookmark
Edit Text Keys:	
BACKSPACE	Delete character to left of cursor
DEL	Delete character at cursor
CTRL+T	Delete remainder of word
INS	Set insert mode on/off
END+ENTER	Insert blank line below cursor position
HOME,CTRL+N	Insert blank line above cursor position
Select Text Keys (prior to Cut, Copy, and Clear):	
SHIFT+ARROWS	Select characters/lines of text in direction of arrow keys
CTRL+SHIFT+HOME	Select from cursor position to beginning of file
CTRL+SHIFT+END	Select from cursor position to end of file
Actions on Selected Text Keys:	
CTRL+INS	Copy selected text to Clipboard
SHIFT+DEL	Delete selected text and copy it to Clipboard
CTRL+Y	Delete current line and copy to Clipboard
CTRL+Q,Y	Delete to end of current line and copy to Clipboard
SHIFT+INS	Insert transferred text from Clipboard into document

CUSTOMIZING MS-DOS

During Startup, MS-DOS uses the commands listed in two files, CONFIG.SYS and AUTOEXEC.BAT, to customize the way MS-DOS operates. These files must be present on the root directory of the start up disk (A or C).

CAUTION: Never erase or edit these files without first making a back-up copy.

About config.sys

Config.sys contains commands that configure (set-up) your system. Typically this file installs device drivers and establishes how MS-DOS will use available memory and files.

Sample commands in a CONFIG.SYS file:

```
FILES=20                                  1)
BUFFERS=30                                2)
DEVICE=HIMEM.SYS                          3)
DEVICE=C:\DOS\EMM386.EXE noems            4)
DEVICEhigh=C:\MOUSE\MOUSE.SYS             5)
```

Explanation of sample CONFIG.SYS commands:

1) Specifies that MS-DOS can open as many as 20 files at one time. (Many applications require a minimum number of open files in order to run.)
2) Specifies amount of memory MS-DOS will use for file transfers. (Changes to the number can increase or decrease the speed of disk file transfers to and from memory.)
3) Loads a program (HIMEM.SYS) that allows MS-DOS to use extended memory (memory above 640K) that can then be used for many purposes.
4) Loads a program (EMM386.EXE) that allow (when used with the "noems" switch) you to load programs into upper memory. (Requires an 80386 processor or higher.)
5) Loads a device program (MOUSE.SYS) into upper memory that provides communication between the system and a mouse input device.

■ *About autoexec.bat*

The Autoexec.bat file contains commands that are AUTOMATICALLY EXECUTED during startup. Create or edit an autoexec.bat file to make a customized startup procedure. Since commands in Autoexec.bat are contained in a file, they have to be typed only once. This file must be located (saved) in the root directory of the startup disk (A:\ or C:\).

Sample commands in an AUTOEXEC.BAT file:

```
ECHO OFF                                 1)
DATE                                     2)
TIME                                     3)
PATH=c:\;c:\DOS;c:\WP51;c:\BATCH         4)
PROMPT = $P                              5)
CD\BATCH                                 6)
TYPE MENU.DAT                            7)
```

Explanation of sample AUTOEXEC.BAT commands:

1) Suppresses command messages.
2) Initiates DATE command.
3) Initiates TIME command.
4) Tells MS-DOS what directories to search for executable files.
5) Tells MS-DOS to show the current directory in the DOS prompt.
6) Changes directory to \BATCH.
7) Types out the contents of the MENU.DAT file to the screen.

About batch files

Batch files are special program files that contain MS-DOS commands. Each command in a batch file is executed by MS-DOS when the batch file name is entered at the DOS prompt. All batch files have a BAT filename extension. Because commands in a batch file are typed once, using batch files can make working with MS-DOS faster, easier, and more reliable.

Creating or editing a batch file

To create or edit a batch file, type EDIT at the DOS prompt or choose Editor from the MS-DOS Shell Program list. When prompted, type the name of the batch file to create or edit. (Include drive and path if necessary, and remember to include a BAT filename extension.) For example, type `c:\batch\bakup.BAT`).

Terminating a batch file

To end a batch file before it finishes, press CTRL+BREAK, then type Y and press ENTER to confirm.

Sample commands in a batch file (MENU.BAT)

```
ECHO OFF                                  1)
CLS                                       2)
CD\BATCH                                  3)
TYPE MENU.DAT                             4)
```

Explanation of sample MENU.BAT commands:

1) Suppresses command messages.
2) Clears the screen.
3) Changes directories (makes \BATCH the current directory).
4) Types out the contents of the MENU.DAT file to the screen.

GLOSSARY

Autoexec.bat A special batch file, located in the root directory of the startup disk, that contains commands executed each time the computer is started.

ASCII file A text file that does not contain format codes.

Backing up The process of duplicating the information stored in files on your computer for safekeeping.

Batch file A text file containing DOS commands and programs to be run.

Booting The initial loading of DOS into memory when the computer is turned on or reset.

Byte A unit of computer storage that is equal to one character.

Command line See "DOS prompt".

Command.com A MS-DOS program file. This file must be present in the root directory of your startup disk.

Current directory The first directory in the directory tree that MS-DOS will look in for external commands or program files. Files in the current directory can be referenced without specifying their directory location. (See "Path".)

Current drive The first drive MS-DOS will look in for external commands or program files. Files in the current drive can be referenced without specifying their drive location.

Data bits A parameter included in the MODE command that set the number of data bits in a character when transmitting data through a serial port.

Default directory See "Current directory".

Default drive See "Current Drive".

Directory A file location where groups of related files are stored.

Directory Tree The structure of directories that branch out from the root directory.

Disk A device used to store data. Information, contained in files, is written on the surface of disks. Also see "Diskette" and "Hard Disk".

Diskette A portable disk that can store anywhere from 360 kilobytes to 1.44 megabytes of data and programs.

DOS Abbreviation for Disk Operating System. DOS is the set of programs that allows your computer to store data, execute programs, and manage your disk drives, keyboard, and screen. MS-DOS is a brand name for a version of DOS provided by Microsoft.

DOS prompt The string of characters that marks the place on the screen where you type the next DOS command. It usually looks something like A>> or C>>. (Also see the "PROMPT command".)

External command A command which must be read into RAM memory from a disk each time it is executed.

File A set of information stored on a disk which can contain data (for example, the inventory file) or a program (the inventory program file).

Filename extension The characters of a filename that follow the period in a filename. For example, in the filename DOSQRG.TXT, the filename extension is TXT. Many programs use the filename extension to categorize files by type.

Fixed disk See "Hard disk".

Floppy disk See "Diskette".

Format Before diskettes can be used for the first time, they must be prepared for use. Formatting diskettes does this. If you format a diskette that already has data on it, all of that data will be erased permanently. (Also see the "FORMAT command".)

Function keys The keys to the left, or along the top, of your keyboard marked "F1", "F2", etc. These keys serve different purposes (functions) depending on the program you are using.

Hard disk A disk that is built into your computer and is not removable. Hard disks can hold from 10 million up to hundreds of millions of bytes of data and programs.

Internal command A command which is built into your computer's memory. Internal commands do not have to be read into RAM memory when they are executed.

K, KB, Kilobyte One thousand bytes. (Also see "Byte".)

Keystroke commands A DOS command that can be performed by pressing just one or two keys.

Logical drive A disk drive that simulates a separate and physical disk drive. For example, one physical drive can be divided into two logical drives.

M, Meg, MB, Megabyte One million bytes. (Also see "Byte".)

Memory See "RAM," "Disk," "Diskette".

Memory resident A type of program that is loaded into RAM memory and stays resident so that it is available to the computer user at all times. Examples of memory resident programs are the DOS PRINT command and the DOS MIRROR command.

Parity A parameter included in the MODE command that sets the error checking procedure used when transmitting data through a serial port.

Path The notation used to specify to DOS a unique subdirectory. It consists of a backslash followed by the names of the higher-level subdirectories, separated by backslashes, leading down to the desired subdirectory. Path is also used loosely to mean Path list, as used in this book. (Also see "Path list".)

Path list A list of directories which DOS searches through for programs and external commands when they are not found in the current directory. The directories in this list are searched in the order they appear in the list. (Also see "Path".)

Program A set of instructions that tells the computer how to perform a specific task. Programs are usually stored in files with the extension EXE or COM.

RAM Random Access Memory; the memory chips which the computer uses to store programs and data while they are being used. The contents of RAM are removed as soon as the computer is turned off.

Retry A parameter included in the MODE command that specifies actions to take when MODE attempts to send data to a printer that is busy.

Root directory The main directory on a disk. All subdirectories are under this directory.

Stop bits A parameter included in the MODE command that set the number of stop bits used to mark the end of a character when data is transmitted through a serial port.

Subdirectory A directory which is a member of a directory. Subdirectories are used to sub-group related sets of files.

Substitution words See the table of substitution words on page 3.

System disk A diskette or hard disk that has the special files needed to start up the computer.

Text editor A program that allows you to create and change the contents of text files. MS-DOS Editor is the text editor that comes with MS-DOS version 5.0.

TSR Abbreviation for Terminate and Stay Resident. See "Memory Resident".

Volume label An optional name that can be given to a diskette or hard disk.

Wildcards Characters that stand for one or more characters of a filename. They allow a single DOS command to operate on many files at once. ? stands for any single character and * stands for any group of characters.

This page intentionally left blank.

INDEX

INDEX

INDEX

INDEX

INDEX

INDEX

At your local bookstore, or directly from us.

Did we make one for you?

	CAT. NO.
AppleWorks (Ver. 2)	A-17
AppleWorks (Ver. 3)	H-17
dBase III Plus	B-17
dBase IV	B-18
DisplayWrite 4	D-4
DOS 5	J-17
First Publisher 3.0	F-17
Lotus 1-2-3	L-17
Lotus 1-2-3 (Ver 2.2)	L2-17
Microsoft Windows 3	N-17
Microsoft Word 5.0	C-17
Microsoft Word 5.5	C-28
Microsoft Works	K-17
Multimate Adv II & Ver 4	G-17
PC & MS DOS	X-17
Professional Write	P-17
Quattro Pro	Q-17
SuperCalc 3	S-17
WordPerfect 4.2	W-17
WordPerfect 5.0	W-5.0
WordPerfect 5.1	W-5.1
WordStar 6.0	R-17

ORDER FORM

Quantity discount for corporate buyers.
Ask for Jane Bond
800-528-3897

Dictation Disc Company
14 East 38 Street, New York, NY 10016

Accept my order for the following titles at $7.95 each.

QTY.	CAT. NO.	DESCRIPTION

( ) I enclose check. Add $2 for postage and handling.

Name ______________________

Address ______________________

City, State, Zip ______________________